Basics of Teaching
for Christians

Other Books by Robert W. Pazmiño

By What Authority Do We Teach?
Foundational Issues in Christian Education (2nd ed.)
Latin American Journey
Principles and Practices of Christian Education
The Seminary in the City

Basics of Teaching for Christians

Preparation, Instruction, and Evaluation

Robert W. Pazmiño

Baker Books

A Division of Baker Book House Co
Grand Rapids, Michigan 49516

To

My daughter, Rebekah Joy Pazmiño, who has often reminded me
of the basics, and members of the teaching course over the years

© 1998 by Robert W. Pazmiño

Published by Baker Books
a division of Baker Book House Company
P.O. Box 6287, Grand Rapids, MI 49516-6287

Printed in the United States of America

ISBN: 0-8010-2173-1

Library of Congress Cataloging-in-Publication data is on file at the Library of
Congress, Washington, D.C.

Scripture citations are from the New Revised Standard Version (NRSV) of the
Bible, copyright 1989 by the Division of Christian Education of the National
Council of the Churches of Christ in the U.S.A. and are used by permission.

For information about academic books, resources for Christian leaders, and
all new releases available from Baker Book House, visit our web site:
http://www.bakerbooks.com

Contents

Introduction

Why write a book for Christians about the basics of teaching? Shouldn't basics apply to all teachers, whether they are Christian or not? In some respects, the answer to this second question is "Yes." Teaching involves certain skills that any person can develop over time. But the perspective that undergirds *this* book is that teaching for Christians is a ministry that calls for partnership with God and attention to Christian distinctives that communicate care. Christians share with others the need to attend to the basics or fundamentals in all areas of life. In a world of increasing complexity, the attention given to basics can help focus one's efforts in spite of distractions. This holds true for teachers and for Christians who hope to see all of life from the perspective of their calling to follow Christ.

The Christian ministry of teaching requires the devotion of persons called by God to make a difference in the lives of individuals, communities, and societies. This ministry is a high calling that necessitates both diligence and the willingness to playfully and creatively explore options for one's teaching. Diligence is required in the planning, implementation, and evaluation of teaching. Diligence is also required in the disciplines of sharing transformative content and listening carefully during one's teaching practice. Listening to persons and discerning dimensions of their context in the process of teaching are essential. As compared with diligence, creativity and playfulness in teaching imply a willingness to risk and to explore creative alternatives to the normal educational fare. Playfulness also implies an openness to the work of the Holy Spirit as serendipitous elements emerge from a variety of sources that include the contributions of participants in the teaching encounter and events in the wider world that call for our attention.

Persons who embrace the Christian faith or, better stated, persons who have been embraced by Jesus Christ, have in the life and ministry of Jesus an exemplar, a model for teaching. Jesus' model is expanded by Christian teachers who stand in the tradition of Jesus, who transformed the lives of his hearers in a variety of ways. Transformative contact with Jesus often included both confrontation with the truth and an experience of love that reached the very depths of one's soul. Contact with the resurrected Christ continues to be the ultimate end of Christian teaching so that persons might glorify and enjoy God now and forever. This glorification and enjoyment does not shy away from the experience of the cross and confronting the suffering of God and others in addressing the human condition of sin. Sin is manifest in the personal and corporate dimensions of life and calls for the ministry of reconciliation with God and all of God's creation (2 Cor. 5:11–6:2). An exploration of teaching with these theological purposes in mind will make connections between this ministry and the larger mission of the Christian church. This larger mission grounds our teaching and provides direction for those who seek to faithfully practice this ministry. Such a connection between teaching and the church's wider mission fosters life, much as the branches depend on the true vine for sustenance (John 15:1–17).

Recognizing the Christian foundations for teaching grounds the efforts of all teachers who acknowledge their continual need for divine help and direction. This acknowledgment calls for an openness to the ministry of the Holy

Spirit in all dimensions of teaching. The Spirit's presence and prodding is a source of encouragement and empowerment in teaching tasks, which can readily become routine and devoid of joy and promise. The Spirit can also guide us into supportive relationships with other teachers. Fellowship that is honest and open can provide perspective as we learn about problems that others have encountered in their teaching ministries. Fellowship also reminds us of the partnership that Christian teachers have with God the Father, Son, and Spirit in their particular ministries. This partnership calls for reliance on prayer prior to, during, and after every teaching occasion.

This work is designed to explore teaching in three phases that can be projected over time. In discussing the process of teaching in my earlier work, *Principles and Practices of Christian Education,* I pointed out that teachers are involved in planning, implementing, and evaluating.[1]

Chapter 1 of this work considers the initial phase of preparation and planning for teaching. In one sense, it takes a lifetime to prepare for any one teaching occasion. But in a more practical sense, specific choices and plans are made prior to one's actual teaching practice. In many cases this may include following a prescribed curriculum and reviewing plans that others have proposed. But even in this case, teachers need to adapt any plan to the particular persons and setting in which they are serving. The designers of any published curriculum do not usually know the individual students in a classroom, whose situation must be considered if connections with the proposed curriculum are to be made. What happens in Juan's or Jane's week can make all the difference in how they respond to a particular prescribed lesson plan. Diligence and sensitivity on the part of individual teachers are called for as they sort through what might be done in their next class session.

Chapter 2 of this work explores the actual practice of teaching, when teachers and students interact in an educational setting. Teaching needs to be playful, precise, and concerned for both process and products. Teaching can be analyzed in relation to a musical metaphor that includes a prelude, a "lude," and a postlude.[2] These three elements have also been suggested in the popular wisdom of presenting instructional content: tell people what you are going to share, share the material itself, and then finally tell them what you did share in review, which leads to either retention or redundancy. Certainly this is not the only approach to teaching that engages participants, but it outlines some important basics.

The third chapter considers the important place of evaluation and reflection on the teaching that has been completed. This task is much too often neglected, but is essential for the faithful practice of teaching. This third phase fosters one's stewardship of a teaching gift and some accountability for the persons under one's care. Teaching can embody a ministry of care for the educational content, care for the persons involved, and care for the context in which persons live. Evaluation can assist us in being more "careful" the next time, or can encourage us to try something different that can be a stretch for us as well as for our students. Evaluation can affirm the teaching gifts entrusted to our personal care and can provide constructive criticism from which all of us can benefit as we strive to live more faithfully as teachers of the Christian faith and as Christians who are teachers in a wide variety of fields and levels of education.

The usual tendency in teaching practice is to focus exclusively on doing, the topic of chapter 2, and the second phase of teaching. But Iris Cully, a wise Christian educator with much experience, points out that "doing requires preparation and the sharing of knowledge and experience."[3] Thus the rush to practice in teaching is best prevented through careful planning and reflection prior to teaching, as will be suggested in chapter 1. Without adequate time and energy invested in the first phase of preparation for teaching, the second phase of actual practice is more problematic. Cully also points out that "reflecting afterward reveals how well the teachers are able to share and where they feel a need to increase their own knowledge and understanding."[4] The third phase of evaluating teaching cannot be ignored by those teachers who view their ministries as a matter of Christian stewardship.

I propose an acronym to encapsulate these three phases of teaching and their corresponding chapters. This acronym was originally used for a cooperative program that began in 1987 between two denominational groups and the theological school where I teach. The acronym is **PIE** and it designates a **P**artnership **I**n **E**ducation that is being forged among local church educational leaders, their statewide denominational bodies, and a theological school that together have sought to foster effective teaching in local churches. That same acronym can also be applied to the three phases of teaching, **p**reparation, **i**nstruction, and **e**valuation, which support faithful teaching in general and in the Christian tradition. To further mix metaphors, "PIE" complements an underlying metaphor I propose for teaching if one thinks of an actual pie that is baked, placed on a table, and shared with others.

The underlying metaphor for this work defines faithful and effective teaching as artfully setting an inviting table that welcomes all to participate and results in joyful celebration. To extend this metaphor, Christian teaching is best portrayed in relation to the Lord's table, where Jesus himself is the host who offers nourishment and life to all who partake, fulfilling the promise of Isaiah 55:1–3a with its invitation to abundant life:

> Ho, everyone who thirsts,
>   come to the waters;
> and you that have no money,
>   come, buy and eat!

> Come, buy wine and milk
>   without money and without price.
> Why do you spend your money for
>   that which is not bread,
> and your labor for that which does
>   not satisfy?
> Listen carefully to me, and eat what
>   is good,
>   and delight yourselves in rich food.
> Incline your ear, and come to me;
>   listen, so that you may live.

At the metaphorical table of teaching, Jesus offers himself as the bread of life (John 6:35, 48), and he offers the living water to all those who thirst (John 4:10–15; 7:37–38). This offer is extended to all those persons who will be served and who in turn are asked to serve others. In addition, this metaphor of the inviting table suggests a crucial relationship between teaching and worship. Faithful teaching can encourage a response of worship to God and a sense of wonder and awe in relation to all of God's creation. But for Christians, creation finds its fulfillment in relation to the revelation of Jesus Christ and his offer of new life to an estranged humanity. Persons alienated from God are now welcomed to Jesus' table just as the father in the New Testament parable welcomed to table fellowship both the prodigal son and the angry, resentful older son for a common meal (Luke 15:11–32). The invitation still needs to be extended through the Christian ministry of teaching by those called to serve Christ today.

A contemporary film that captures the transformative power of the well-prepared and presented meal is *Babette's Feast*. This film portrays the costly and creative efforts of a stranger in a remote village who expresses her gratitude to others by serving a dinner to which all are invited. She lavishly expends an inheritance she has received to prepare the meal, which has an amazing impact on her guests. Maxine Greene, an existential educational philosopher, suggests that teachers can serve as provocative strangers who foster a sense of wonder with their students.[5] It is the author's hope that those who teach will embrace the spirit portrayed in this film through their ministries. Even though initially strangers to their students, Christian teachers can extend an invitation to feast at a table Jesus has hosted throughout time and into eternity.

It is appropriate for me to express here special appreciation to one of my students. I thank Lesley Woo, who was a member of the teaching course I taught in 1996 and who also served as a teaching assistant. Lesley provided insightful comments on and editorial recommendations for the initial drafts of this work that greatly improved its presentation. Teachers have much to learn from those with whom they minister. Special thanks is also extended to the members of the "Teaching: Principles and Practices" course I taught in 1996. Their encouragement and the quality of their own teaching ministries contributed to the writing of this work.

Preparation

As suggested in the introduction to this work, the preparation for teaching requires adequate attention by teachers if all that follows is to fulfill its greatest potential for transformation in the lives of participants.[1] This preparation calls for each teacher to be committed to paying careful attention on a variety of levels of her or his ministry. Such attention includes planning for the content, persons, and context of teaching while relying on the gracious working of the Holy Spirit throughout the processes of planning and instruction. From the perspective of the Christian faith, this suggests the need for a partnership in teaching between the human teacher and the Divine Teacher, God. The apostle Paul describes this divine–human partnership in relation to the work of salvation that can also apply to the ministry of teaching: "work out your own salvation with fear and trembling; for it is God who is at work in you, enabling you both to will and to work for his good pleasure" (Phil. 2:12b–13). Teachers are called on to recognize the mystery of their ministries where God is at work along with areas for which they are directly responsible and accountable for the hard work of careful and creative preparation. Teachers are stewards of the gifts and abilities they have received from God for the sharing of content and the shaping of persons who are under their care. This shaping does not presume the determinative character of teaching, but the offering of possibilities that the students or participants also need to own if any change is to be realized as a result of teaching. Students need to work out the meaning and implications of the teaching they receive as God also works in their lives to accomplish God's purposes through their active and receptive learning of the content.

As a result of the cooperative nature of teaching by Christians that includes the ministry of God's Spirit and the active participation of students, preparation for teaching calls for active reliance on God's wisdom as revealed in the Scriptures and the person of Jesus Christ along with the living traditions of those who have gone before us in their own teaching ministries. By acknowledging and affirming this reliance, the teacher serves as a representative of a larger community that includes the Trinity, as God in three persons teaches humanity, and the host of teachers of the Christian faith down through the ages. The very collaborative nature of Christian teaching also calls for the teacher to carefully discern and consider in planning what is happening in the lives of students. This consideration explores what students bring to the teaching occasion, how they interact during the actual instruction, and where teachers hope they will transfer their learning in the present and future application of what is learned to life. Consideration by teachers of these three dimensions of the students' world serves to weave together the three phases of preparation, instruction, and evaluation that are basic to teaching itself. In this way a teacher can potentially engage the students in learning that parallels the teaching activities as they were planned for and implemented. Such a consideration implies the viewing of teaching as a conjoint journey in which a map is designed, but the actual experience of both students and teachers may be quite distinct from initial expectations.

Teaching from this vantage point calls for an openness to the unexpected along with a commitment to follow a predetermined plan wherever it is possible. Game plans are necessary, but circumstances may require a change of plans. Therefore teachers are called on to recognize a paradox in teaching: there is a need for careful planning and a need for flexibility in implementing plans. For teachers this requires the taking of risks in planning and a realistic acknowledgment of the possibility of failure in the actual instruction. Some students, despite the best-laid plans, may fail to learn and some teachers may not witness the long hoped for transformation in the perspectives and lives of those under their care. Faced with this situation, the Christian teacher ultimately is called on to entrust her or his students into the care of God and to the transformation that God's Spirit alone can realize in human hearts and minds. Here the partnership between human teachers and the Divine Teacher takes on reality as we recognize the limits of our efforts and the greater work of God within the lives of both students and their teachers.

As a result of their divine partnership, Christian teachers are called to recognize their dependence on God from the initial stages of responding to the call to teach. Discerning the promptings of the Holy Spirit requires a daily encounter with the living God who speaks to us through the Scriptures, prayer, the created order, and a variety of relationships. In an increasingly fast-paced world, an encounter with God the Spirit requires time apart for reflection and receptivity in both the rush and heat of the day and the calm and quiet of the night. No easy formulas exist for how the Spirit works with the varied textures of our human hearts and the variety of ways in which we as persons learn and in turn teach. For some of us, God only can get our attention with dramatic events that stop us in our tracks and cause us to look beyond ourselves toward heaven. For others of us, discernment is possible in the faint whispers that punctuate our careful listening in depth and on various levels to what is happening in and around us. For still others, our daily encounters with other persons and other creatures serve to draw our attention to God's lessons and perspectives that all too readily have been forgotten or ignored in the rush to accomplish our written and unwritten agendas. Little wonder, then, that teaching may fail to have a lasting impact or meet the deep hunger of hearts and minds for truths to enrich and guide our lives.

While recognizing the risks of teaching devoid of transformative possibility, teachers can strive to pass on a living faith and vital content that connects with lives of persons with implications for the contexts where they live, move, and have their being (Acts 17:28). Along with the apostle Paul and the Athenians, we as teachers can recognize that it is in God that we live, move, and have our being. What follows from this insight is that our teaching also is called to have its life, movement, and being in God. How in the world is this possible? A further exploration of the preparation for teaching will serve to consider that question and its implications for how we approach our teaching ministries with a renewed sense of God's presence and delight along with a wonder regarding what God continues to accomplish through the foolishness of teaching not unlike the foolishness of preaching (1 Cor. 1:21). The Book of Acts describes the yoked ministries of teaching and preaching that characterized the New Testament church (Acts 5:42; 15:35) and that have continued through the Christian era. The ministry of teaching requires careful attention to the matter of preparation.

The Matter of Preparation

Preparation for teaching calls for the best of one's critical and creative energies as a teacher. Thought regarding preparation is not new in the history of Christian ministry or educational thought. The Puritans developed a doctrine of preparation that focused on the preparation of the heart for the gracious working of God's Spirit, which is also the goal of Christian teaching.[2] But a contemporary example of this matter of preparation can also be drawn from the culinary arts, which is the area of work my son is exploring as his vocation after his graduate study in the field of history. In a number of ways, my proposed definition of teaching as setting the feast on the table has a definite affinity with the art of cooking and the following example.

While preparing a recent Thanksgiving feast for the gathered extended family, my son, David, announced the menu that included, of all things, Brussels sprouts. He had just completed six months of culinary school and hoped to share with us some of what he had learned, even to the extent of providing a printed menu with all the recipes our meal entailed. My mother and my sister and her family had traveled from the New York City area to join us for Thanksgiving in Newton, Massachusetts. My youthful memories of Brussels sprouts were *not* positive. These miniature cabbages brought to mind the thought that they were only edible when covered with ample quantities of butter and salt. My father, who loved to cook on the weekends and for church suppers, was fond of bitter vegetables. But I just couldn't imagine Brussels sprouts as a welcome addition to our table on, of all days, Thanksgiving.

In discussing the matter with my wife, we approached our son and asked subtly and diplomatically about the Brussels sprouts. (One learns to deal circumspectly with a chef in questioning culinary creations.) David's response was that we never had tasted *his* Brussels sprouts, which was true. Though not thoroughly convinced, we were willing at least to give them a try, especially as they were identified as "Sautéed Brussels Sprouts with Crispy Pancetta" on our carefully printed family menu. Because I volunteered to be the preparation assistant for the chef, I was able to observe the preparation of the Brussels sprouts firsthand. Part of the preparation called for me to use a melon scoop to remove the bitter center from each sprout and to carefully separate each of the leaves. My son explained that coring the sprouts removed the bitter portion. I was beginning to learn! The pancetta, an Italian bacon, was prepared in a pan and at the right moment the Brussels sprout leaves and appropriate seasonings were added. The pan was covered, and the sprouts were cooked for the allotted time. David pointed out to me that the finished dish and its presentation were dependent on the careful preparation of the sprouts, not my memories of those bitter vegetables that were difficult to swallow. I was almost convinced. Of course, the fruit of these efforts awaited the reception of the dish along with all the other special items on our menu that made for an exquisite gourmet meal. To our great surprise, the first dish to disappear was the Brussels sprouts.[3] In fact, our thirteen-year-old daughter, who is particularly selective in her eating habits, had four servings. When I returned to one of my Christian education classes, which earlier had been informed about the upcoming menu for our Thanksgiving meal, the students asked how the Brussels sprouts had fared. I was delighted to report the results and what I had learned from my son. The preparation made all the difference in that dish.

This example points up the need for careful preparation—not only in the arena of the culinary arts, but also in the teaching arts, which require a commitment of time and energy prior to the actual presentation of any lesson. Preparation for teaching can be explored first in relation to the teachers themselves and then in relation to the students, the content, and the context for teaching. All of these areas of preparation can be related to the metaphor of teaching as setting a table. In the teaching of Christians, this setting of a table relates to the basic question, How do we set the table for the Holy Spirit? The Spirit is the active presence of God, who transforms the efforts of the teacher into life-changing events for the students. To be present at table, teachers are called on to consider their preparation.

The preparation of the teacher involves the heart, the spirit or soul, the mind, and the body or strength of the teacher. The categories of heart, soul, mind, and strength will be recognized as those named in the first of two great commandments found in the Scriptures ("the mind" is not identified in the First [or Old] Testament passage of Deuteronomy 6:5, but mentioned in the Second [or New] Testament passages of Matthew 22:37, Mark 12:30, and Luke 10:27).[4] One implication of associating the preparation for teaching with the love of God is that such preparation can be viewed as an act of love and a form of worship that seeks to give glory to God. Preparation can be an expression of loving care for the ministry of teaching to which one is called by God. The second of the two great commandments, loving one's neighbor as oneself, can be associated with the care of preparation for one's students, for the context in which the teaching is planned to occur, and for the content of the teaching itself. In this case, one's students can be viewed as neighbors during the time of interaction with a teacher. The same categories of heart, soul, mind, and strength can be applied to students or participants in the teaching.

The preparation of the content that is associated with lesson planning can expand on the normal association of content with cognitive content to include affective, behavioral, intentional, and spiritual content that incorporates both individual and corporate or cooperative dimensions. The preparation of the context brings to attention the settings for learning and the various environmental variables that researchers of teaching have identified for consideration. Loving attention to the context of teaching is also a responsibility of the teacher. But the initial challenge for the teacher is to attend to herself or himself in the process of preparation that includes the heart, soul or spirit, mind, and strength or body. This is a matter of immediate but also eternal significance in a Christian approach.

Preparation of the Teacher's Heart

The Scriptures have repeated references to matters of the heart. Proverbs 4:23 shares the following wisdom: "Keep your heart with all vigilance, for from it flow the springs of life." Teachers are called on to keep and set their hearts so that life can issue forth in their teaching. In this commitment, teachers recognize that God does not look on one's outward appearance, but on the heart of a person (1 Sam. 16:7). This wisdom of considering heart matters corresponds with Jesus' diagnosis of the human condition as recorded in Mark 7:21–23: "For it is from within, from the human heart, that evil intentions come: fornication, theft, murder, adultery, avarice, wickedness, deceit, licentiousness, envy, slander, pride, folly. All these evil things come from within, and they defile a person." Sin is a reality of the human condition and can impact the ministry of teaching just as it does every other activity in which persons engage. We do not normally associate the sins that Jesus identifies with teaching, but the potential for distortion of truth and life exists in any relationship in which one hopes to model and pass on to others truths and values that can issue in the fullness of life. The Scriptures warn of the influence of false teachers and their impact on the life of the community and individuals who need to encounter the truth of God and to experience the love of God in its various expressions (2 Peter 2:1).

This also can be a lesson drawn from the New Testament Book of James, which is concerned with the congruence of faith and works. Teaching from the heart is a high calling and a responsibility that should only be entered into after careful consideration.[5] This is the suggestion of the writer of the Book of James: "Not many of you should become teachers, my brothers and sisters, for you know that we who teach will be judged with greater strictness" (3:1). The privilege of teaching has a corresponding responsibility to prepare and guard one's heart because it is from the heart that transformative teaching can flow as teachers are instruments of the living God. In the Christian faith the calling to teach involves a decision to follow Jesus in one's teaching. Such a decision is a matter of the heart.

As mentioned above, the Puritans were concerned about the preparation of one's heart for the Christian life.[6] In their ministry, teachers are called to prepare for God's grace to work first in their own hearts, and then in the hearts of their students. This preparation involves a conscious turning to God in prayer and an introspective examination of the center of one's life from which life can flow. In addition to Philippians 2:12–13, the Puritans referred to 2 Peter 1:10 to provide scriptural warrant for such examination: "Therefore, brothers and sisters, be all the more eager to confirm your call and election, for if you do this, you will never stumble." This examination is not a morbid preoccupation, but a reminder of the nature of one's ministry and accountability to God. It also serves as a reminder to be diligent in one's efforts as an expression of devotion to God. One exemplar of such devotion is Ezra, who expressed his devotion in three areas as described in Ezra 7:10: "For Ezra had set his heart to study the law of the LORD, and to do it, and to teach the statutes and ordinances in Israel." This was a matter of the heart that served to clarify one's commitments and the investment of one's time and energies. The issue of commitment and devotion is still central in the ministry of teaching. Ezra was a priest and scribe whom Jewish tradition designates as "the second Moses," but he is an example to Christian teachers who are members of the priesthood of all believers identified in 1 Peter 2:1–10.[7]

In the exploration of the preparation of the heart, the Puritans recognized that God enabled this preparation to occur as persons were open to the gracious promptings of God's Spirit in their hearts. The responsibility of the Christian teacher is to be open and receptive even when circumstances are disheartening and distracting. A conscious turning to God, an asking for wisdom, direction, and sensitivity to oneself, one's students, the content to be shared, and the context for teaching is essential. To return to our table imagery, we set the table and leave a chair open for the hoped-for guest as we are to attentively listen and open ourselves for dialogue on crucial issues related to our teaching.[8] In Jewish tradition that guest is Elijah, but in the Christian tradition it is Jesus who is welcome at the table of our hearts for fellowship and interaction on the journey of teaching, just as his disciples encountered him on the road to Emmaus (Luke 24:13–35). This implies the openness of the teacher's heart to God's work and will through the ministry of teaching. In this way, the teacher sets the table for the gracious presence and work of the Holy Spirit. As a result of the preparation of the teacher's heart, his or her personality can become a means for instruction. Abraham Heschel observed that "It is the personality of the teacher which is the text that the pupils read; the text that they will never forget."[9]

An openness to heart matters may raise the issue of sin within the lives of us who serve as teachers as suggested by Jesus' words recorded in Mark 7:21–23. Though not a popular topic in most educational circles, sin is a factor that impacts life in general and any teaching effort. The prophet Joel offers a helpful perspective on sin that calls for the rending of our hearts in a response of repentance before God: "Yet even now, says the LORD, return to me with all your heart, with fasting, with weeping, and with mourning; rend your hearts and not your clothing. Return to the LORD, your God, for he is gracious and merciful, slow to anger, and abounding in steadfast love, and relents from punishing" (Joel 2:12–13).

With the recognition of sin can also come the reception of God's remedy for sin in the life, death, and resurrection of Jesus Christ. Therefore the preparation of one's heart may call for its. . . . . to deal with unconfessed sin. Such rendering can heed the warning and promise of 1 John 1:8–10: "If we say that we have no sin, we deceive ourselves, and the truth is not in us. If we confess our sins, he who is faithful and just will forgive our us our sins and cleanse us from all unrighteousness. If we say that we have not sinned, we make him a liar, and his word is not in us." The confession of sin that comes with the rendering of the heart provides the occasion for God to prepare the heart of the teacher for the challenges of teaching. Such confession may also involve asking the forgiveness of students or others if they were offended by the teacher's actions or attitudes. The preparation of the teacher's heart may involve not only a rendering, but through forgiveness and cleansing an empowerment by God's Spirit for renewed efforts that can be transformative for all those involved.

Preparation of the Teacher's Spirit

The mention of God's Spirit and the Spirit's work in human hearts raises the question of the place of the teacher's spirit or soul that is engaged in the preparation for teaching. A discussion of the teacher's heart and spirit as separate categories may lead to a fragmented view of the person of the teacher, who needs to be seen as a whole and not reduced to isolated dimensions. A fragmented view of persons is a danger to be avoided in relation to teachers and students. While recognizing this danger, a consideration of the teacher's spirit can serve to introduce the important issue of the teacher's spirituality or spiritual life as it impacts the preparation for the ministry of teaching. In exploring the spiritual ministry of teaching, it will be helpful to define Christian spirituality in an age of diverse spiritualities and then consider the work of four Christian educators.

With various understandings of spirituality proposed in current discussions, I prefer the perspective that Augustine, the great teacher of the Christian church, offered. Augustine believed that everyone has an order of loves that serves to guide their actions in life.[10] The order of one's loves is central to the Christian faith as stated in the two great commandments, loving God with all our heart, soul, mind, and strength, and loving our neighbors as ourselves. Because of the presence of sin in human persons, fulfilling these commandments is an impossibility save for the provision God has made for humanity in the person of Jesus Christ and in the continuing ministry of the Holy Spirit in the realm of human hearts and community. From the perspective of the Christian faith, a discussion of spirituality without reference to the person and work of the Holy Spirit in relationship to human spirits is bankrupt and misdirected. Love is poured into our hearts through the Holy Spirit who has been given to Christians (Rom. 5:5). God has created persons with the capacity for communion and relationship on the spiritual level that finds fulfillment in the love of God and one's neighbor.

The ultimate purpose of human life is to glorify and enjoy God forever. This truth has been affirmed by a host of Christian confessions and catechisms over the years, and made explicit in the Westminster Confession of 1646. Except for more recent popular usage, historically the spiritual life of persons was referred to as "piety" or "devotion," with the object of one's piety or devotion being God. In current discussions, spirituality is too often focused on the individual spiritual life divorced from both historical and communal moorings—and even from God. The reductionism and spiritual bankruptcy of a Christian spiritual quest divorced from the Holy Spirit and the community of believers that the Holy Spirit formed at Pentecost are apparent. Such a warning does not discount the genuine spiritual hunger that exists in wider society, but points up how historical sources can satisfy that hunger in the Christian faith and support the glorious gospel of Jesus Christ.

One of the four educators who provides insights for preparation of teachers' spirits is James Loder. In *The Knight's Move,* Loder draws on an illustration from the work of Søren Kierkegaard, who described the relationship between the Holy Spirit and the human spirit in terms of the move of a knight on a chessboard. The knight is unlike any other chess piece in that it can move in two directions at right angles and has the distinct advantage of being able to jump over other pieces on the board. In an actual chess game, the knight's move may be unexpected and surprising to the player who has not anticipated the possible consequences of its moves. The "knight of faith" in human life is the Holy Spirit, who encounters human spirits in what can also be described as unexpected and surprising ways. The encounter with the Holy Spirit brings persons into communion with God, the very Creator of life. This encounter quickens their spirit and brings life in its fullness to human experience. In relationship with the human spirit, the Holy Spirit brings renewal and transformation, satisfying the deepest of hungers.[11] The hope of Christian teachers can include the sharing of resources to address the spiritual hunger of students even while sharing content in a wide variety of subject matters.

How does the knight's move, the person and work of the Holy Spirit, influence the preparation of the teacher's spirit for the ministry of teaching? No easy formulas can be proposed that parallel the intense development of a chess master and chess strategy. But teachers are encouraged to be open to what the Spirit has done and is doing in the lives of all the participants in a teaching ministry when planning to teach. This openness is facilitated through times of prayer that involve active listening and meditation along with the necessary amount of time required for germinating new ideas, skills, and sensitivities. Planning may also consider the addition of creative or critical learning experiences that were not previously attempted while considering the risks of such ventures. Teaching is risky business, yet launching out in new ventures or reviving some long forgotten teaching approaches may open new options for students. Teachers are also encouraged to consider the serendipitous elements that can arise in any particular class session that will call for a change in what might be planned in subsequent gatherings of a particular group or proposed for later programming by other teachers. In my formal teaching responsibilities, I plan to arrive at class at least fifteen minutes before the regular set-up requirements of a room would dictate for the express purpose of interacting with students as they arrive and considering, in principle, the possibility of changes that may be already outlined as options in a lesson plan. Options are often planned in relation to the varying risks or alternative directions for student or participant learning.

A second educator whose work has implications for the preparation of the teacher's spirit is Richard Osmer, who wrote *A Teachable Spirit* in which he follows John Calvin in maintaining that at the very heart of Christian piety stands a teachable spirit.[12] The title of Osmer's work is suggestive of the perspective required of all those who would teach in the Christian tradition. Teachers are called on to have a teachable spirit in the sense of being open to learn and curious to discover new insights or make new connections not previously apparent. This also suggests that teachers need to be open to what students may offer or pose in terms of questions to consider either immediately or in subsequent teaching plans. The questions that students ask in class for which I do have a partial or incomplete answer provide the occasion for my learning or undertaking conjoint research with the students between class sessions. What I am suggesting is a stance of mutuality in the planning for teaching that allows for dialogue and welcomes the questions posed by participants even if they are initially perceived as diverting attention from the topic at hand. The teacher should not have such tight scheduling in a plan that no time exists for the digestion of material, the wrestling with implications or applications, and the raising of critical questions. Certainly some questioning can be a creative diversion from key content that students need to master, but in general the inquiries of students need to be accommodated in the plans that teachers develop.

A third educator who explores the preparation for teaching in relation to the role of the spirit is Mary Elizabeth Mullino Moore. Moore proposes seven aspects of teaching from the heart:

1. Teaching is revering God—giving reverence to the spirit and source of life.
2. Teaching is revering the other—other persons, other cultures, other parts of the environment.
3. Teaching is revering oneself.
4. Teaching is revering relationships along various dimensions.
5. Teaching is revering the vocation of teaching—the vocation to nourish the body and receive and replenish the depleted blood.
6. Teaching is revering the process of education itself, including the rhythms of the educational process.
7. Teaching is revering the ordinary.[13]

The spirit that Moore proposes for consideration for teachers is that of reverence along the seven dimensions she outlines. Teachers are called on to embrace a worldview that celebrates the wonder, awe, and joy possible in knowing God the Father, honoring God the Son, and walking with God the Spirit. In terms of preparation, teachers are invited to nurture a relationship with the Triune God, who delights to commune at table with those who seek such fellowship. It is essential to note that the first aspect of teaching that Moore notes is revering God.

With a similar concern, Robin Smith, a fourth educator, maintains that teaching reverence is both a theological and educational necessity. Smith considers reverence to be a feeling of profound respect often mingled with awe and affection. She proposes four theological principles that can make a difference in the planning for and practice of teaching. The four principles are vulnerability, creativity, grace, and dialogue.[14] Before teaching reverence to students, teachers are called on to cultivate reverence for God in their daily walk and to attend to the movements of God's Spirit that bring refreshment and renewal to the human spirit. As applied to the preparation of teachers, they are called on to be vulnerable to God through prayer and meditation while planning; to be open to creative possibilities that can engage the creativity of participants; to be receptive to God's grace in its various forms in their own lives and in the lives of their students that can be shared in the teaching itself; and to plan for dialogue in the actual teaching event, which requires sufficient time and space.

The great Jewish teacher Abraham Joshua Heschel came to a conclusion similar to the insights of the four Christian educators cited above. He observed that "To educate means to cultivate the soul, not only the mind. You cultivate the soul by cultivating empathy and reverence for others, by calling attention to the grandeur and mystery of all being, to the holy dimension of human existence, by teaching how to relate the common to the spiritual."[15] No easy formulas can be proposed for how this can be done given the distinctive faith gifts and sensitivities of each teacher, but the preparation of one's soul or spirit is foundational to transformative teaching. The art of teaching and preparation for the practice of this art call for the nurture of the spirit and soul of the teacher in communion with God and a daily filling with the Holy Spirit. This filling is occasioned by inviting the Spirit to work in one's life and a patient waiting on the Spirit who moves as the wind and blows where it chooses (John 3:8). Isaiah 50:4 suggests that patient waiting requires listening: "The Lord GOD has given me the tongue of a teacher, that I may know how to sustain the weary with a word. Morning by morning he wakens—wakens my ear to listen as those who are taught." Such listening involves the teacher's mind as well as the spirit.

Preparation of the Teacher's Mind

Teaching primarily appeals to the minds of students, though their feelings and wills are also engaged in effective learning. One standard for the Christian teacher's mind is proposed by the apostle Paul in his letter to the Romans: "Do not be conformed to this world, but be transformed by the renewing of your minds, so that you may discern what is the will of God—what is good and acceptable and perfect" (Rom. 12:2). Paul makes another suggestion to the believers in Philippi: "Let the same mind be in you that was in Christ Jesus, who, though he was in the form of God, did not regard equality with God as something to be exploited, but emptied himself, taking the form of a slave, being born in human likeness. And being found in human form, he humbled himself and became obedient to the point of death—even death on a cross" (Phil. 2:5–8). The transformation and renewal of our minds and their being attuned to the mind of Christ depend on our relationship with the Holy Spirit, the Spirit of Christ. The process by which this occurs is best described in 2 Corinthians 3. In this passage, Paul describes how ministers of the new or second covenant function. How they function has implications for the preparation for teaching.

Second Corinthians addresses a number of issues in a teaching ministry. It is known for being disjointed in terms of its arguments, not unlike the creative ambiguity one may confront in a classroom or other teaching setting. Conflicts and problems characterized the Corinthian setting, with different styles and various elements interfacing. This is not unlike teaching with diverse learning styles and perspectives represented. The main point of this passage is to recognize that the Holy Spirit is the agent of transformation in life, which certainly includes the mind as the primary focus of education. In verse 3, persons are compared with a letter written by the Spirit of the living God on tablets of human hearts. The relation of the heart to the mind is an area to consider in planning to teach. In verse 6, life itself is associated with the Spirit in contrast with a reliance on the letter that does not issue in life. In preparing for teaching, teachers need to consider how the proposed content impacts life—the life of the students and the life of the teacher. In this regard, the teacher can consider the connections that can be made with life.[16] Verse 8 describes the ministry of the Spirit as one that comes in glory associated with God's presence and revelation that issues in honor and praise being given to God. This is a potential for any area of academic study that explores the wonder and majesty of God's creation. Verse 17 states that "the Lord is the Spirit, and where the Spirit of the Lord is, there is freedom." Freedom of inquiry and thought is one hallmark of effective teaching as students develop a capacity for critical thought across the life span. In preparing to teach, this ideal can be translated into times to consider diverse perspectives and to dialogue with the posing of critical questions for consideration. Verse 18 mentions the possibility of transformation that is intrinsic to the call to teach, where the minds of participants embrace new possibilities for themselves and the wider community.

Beyond the insights of 2 Corinthians, teachers can recognize that the Spirit is illuminating their minds in their daily efforts. Normal and even in some cases abnormal thought (in a prophetic sense) can be viewed as a gift from God for teaching. Through the everyday preparation in study for teaching and reflection on the what, why, where, when, and how of a plan for teaching, teachers can acknowledge the presence and illumination of God's Spirit.[17] Richard Baxter (1615–91), the seventeenth-century English Presbyterian pastor, affirmed this view of teaching in his *Autobiography* when he observed: "I afterward perceived that education is God's ordinary way for the conveyance of his grace, and ought no more to be set in opposition to the Spirit than the preaching of the Word."[18] The ordinary preparation for teaching as the teacher thinks out options and the normal progression of learning for the students can be an expression of God's grace, care, and providence in the human situation. Of course, the teacher is not to squelch the extraordinary insight that God's Spirit may suggest or supply. My own practice is to keep a blank pad of paper and a pencil on the night table adjacent to my bed to record any inspirational insights that may occur to me at various times in the night. The pencil is preferred to a pen so that I can erase some jottings that should not see the light of day. The teacher must not dismiss the presence of inspiration in the ordinary process of following a syllabus and developing lesson plans that systematically guide students into new territory.

Preparation of the Teacher's Body

The apostle Paul raises a question for the believers at Corinth that is appropriate to pose for teachers: "Do you not know that your body is a temple of the Holy Spirit within you, which you have from God, and that you are not your own?" (1 Cor. 6:19). The following verse provides further expansion: "For you were bought with a price; therefore glorify God in your body." The teacher's body, like any other human body, can become a vehicle used by God to advance God's purposes in the world. The use of one's body to God's ends brings glory to God, who created the human person

33

with all of the wonder and mystery of bodily existence. Therefore, the body of the teacher needs to be considered in the preparation for teaching. How is this possible?

Teachers need to attend to the normal bodily functions of rest, nourishment, exercise, and activity. In a world where stress and nonstop activity is the norm, teachers can model a disciplined or ordered life that allows for the place of ardor, silence, and joy. Times of activity need to be balanced with times of receptivity. Teachers, like others in the Western context, need time to experience sabbath rest without the societal norm of nervous haste. The demands of others can quickly crowd out any time for the most significant other of God, allowing no regular time for prayer, Bible reading, and meditation. Time for others outside the teaching context, and even time for oneself, can be sacrificed because of too many other demands. This can especially occur with a sense of call to teaching that has required a redirection of one's life commitments and vocation. Sometimes the teacher tries to make up for lost time, succumbing to a messianic complex that refuses to set boundaries and maintain limits. Eventually, one's body pays the price of misplaced priorities and a neglect of physical needs. The need for balance is evident in all areas of life, including bodily care.

In seminary teaching I have found it is necessary to plan regular times for rest and recreation that include exercise. Without such attention my body is not capable of responsiveness and receptivity during actual teaching times. A full-time teaching ministry can be taxing if diligence is practiced in preparation and if responsiveness to students is valued. In my situation, teaching competes with committee work, outside ministry demands that include local church and denominational activities, time for writing books like this one, and all-important family time. The demands of teaching in other settings or teaching as a volunteer (which was my experience for five years before beginning seminary studies back in 1975) can include a host of time pressures with multiple choices to be made on a daily basis. All this results in our bodies being pulled in a variety of directions, all of which cannot possibly be fulfilled. What I have discovered over the years is the need to periodically take stock of where one's body is invested and get some feedback regarding the fruits or effects of one's choices. With increased age, one is also aware of the need to work smart in relation to one's body so as to conserve energy and to invest in ways that embrace eternal values beyond the immediate press for urgency that characterizes the general culture in the United States.

Preparation of the Students

In defining teaching metaphorically as the art of setting a table that welcomes all the participants to a joyful cele-bration, it is essential to consider the preparation of the guests who will sit at that table. How the guests are invited and the nature of their expectations make a difference in their actual experience at table and what they will take with them from the occasion. The teacher is also to consider what the participants themselves bring to the table in terms of their experiences, thoughts, and feelings that are shared dur-ing the table fellowship. What is often remembered from a special meal is the conversation that occurred during and after a meal, when people linger and open their hearts and minds in their interactions. This assumes that dialogue and interaction are key elements to anticipate and plan for in ad-vance of the actual teaching. These elements serve to pro-mote the digestion or ownership of the table offerings while recognizing the diverse needs and ways of appropriating what teachers hope to share.

How is it possible to prepare participants for what one wants to teach? In the structure of a class or course the ob-vious avenues for this preparation include an outline or syl-labus that serves to identify the topic of the day and any assignments that students should attend to prior to the particular session. Reading or other assignments can serve to set the stage for actual teaching time along with any questions, problems, or issues that pique the curiosity and interest of students who may also be asked to share what they have learned from their independent or cooperative inquiry prior to the actual session. If any assignments are given, it is important to incorporate feedback into the actual plans. The one occasion I failed to do this in sixteen years of teaching was remembered by students in evaluating a course even though I apologized for my oversight in a subsequent session.

Beyond the obvious place of assignments, I have found that regularly praying for each of the participants I will be teaching serves to help me as a teacher to be better attuned to how a particular lesson or teaching event can connect with the lives of my students. Such prayer also centers on the hoped-for presence and work of the Holy Spirit in the hearts and minds of the participants. I have been humbled over the years that students will recall not those elements clearly outlined in my detailed lesson plan, but the unplanned insights, illustrations, or stories that emerge from the content—which I attribute to the work of the Holy Spirit in making connections to the lives of my students. This points up the relationship between the preparation of the teacher and that of the students in terms of a lifelong walk with the Holy Spirit. In a real sense, it takes a lifetime to prepare for the ministry of teaching that also impacts the lives of students and considers their preparation. In one sense this appears to be overwhelming, but in another sense it frees up teachers to share not only their doctrine or teaching, but also their lives with their students. This is what the apostle Paul suggests in passing on his wisdom to younger ministers in 1 Thessalonians 2:8 and 1 Timothy 4:16.

One other technique I have used over the years is to build anticipation for an upcoming teaching occasion. I do this by mentioning to students what can be expected the following week and how it relates to the current focus so that they can see the unfolding connections. It is also often the case that students themselves raise questions or share insights that directly relate to upcoming teaching content. This is the opportunity to affirm their anticipation and to preview the journey that has been mapped out. It is also the case that students' questions may necessitate a diversion from the course plan, and signaling this possibility can also engage students in preparation for what will follow. This is particularly helpful when the teacher needs to do additional study or research to respond to an inquiry that cannot be answered on the spot. This models for students the cooperative and collaborative nature of teaching and learning, which calls for a partnership between teachers and students. The terms of that partnership invite students to actively prepare and look forward to the actual teaching event and the interaction that is honored there.

An additional dynamic that serves to encourage the active preparation of students is the use of students as presenters or assistants. I have practiced this in children's church sessions, Sunday school classes, teacher training workshops, and seminary courses. The ability of participants to engage teaching content can be enhanced by observing the role of peers who model commitment and serve as bridge persons for what can sometimes be experienced as a chasm between the teacher and the students. Teachers are called on to breach that chasm through the development of personal knowledge of and relationships with students, but there are limits to this possibility that vary with the size of classes and the availability of both teachers and students. A peer who is more experienced in a certain subject area or more advanced in age or level of study can serve effectively to answer individual questions, to help integrate content with the students' realities, and to share content in both provocative and transformative ways that are not accessible to the teacher. This mediating role can make the difference between a good course and one that is excellent in quality and impact on the lives of students. The additional factor that operates in this situation is the mentoring of students who may someday become teachers themselves. I personally have found that this ministry with teaching assistants is essential to fulfill the principle delineated in 2 Timothy 2:2: "and what you have heard from me through many witnesses entrust to faithful people who will be able to teach others as well."

Examples of this discipling principle emerge from my local church ministry experience in teaching and youth ministry. One practice I followed during my ministry in East Harlem, New York, from 1972 to 1975 at the Second Spanish Baptist Church was to have teaching assistants who would work with me in teaching a class. After one or two years, I would leave the class in their hands and move on to another class. This process of discipling and mentoring other teachers involved gradually increasing the assistants' participation in teaching, with regular times for planning and evaluation of each new responsibility. Over time, this ministry also involved an actual teacher training course that met after church on Sunday with a meal and child care provided.

A second outgrowth of this effort at the same local church following my seminary study included the formation of a group of persons committed to youth ministry who met in our home for six sessions on Friday evenings for training that included the planning and evaluation of two actual youth group meetings. A number of the participants were former Sunday school students and youth group members. After seminary and during doctoral studies I had anticipated that my family and I would be leaving the New York area and that we could not resume the same responsibilities for youth and Christian education ministries that I had prior to theological study. We prayed for persons to be open to receive training, and after one year's time twelve persons had signed a covenant with the church to complete the youth leadership training. The fruits of this second effort included the decision of five persons to pursue seminary study and the formation of a youth ministry team in our local church.

A third outgrowth of the ministry was a course on youth leadership that was team taught with a former youth group participant, who by 1978 had completed college and begun seminary studies where I had begun doctoral work. This course, which we team taught in 1979, included youth who were serving as leaders in Hispanic churches throughout the New York City area. A particular joy of this ministry is to note that two of those former students were recently cited in a *Christianity Today* article as key national Christian leaders under the age of forty.[19] One of these brothers was the co-teacher in the course and his brother was a participant. The ministries of these two former students have gone beyond my dreams as they have launched out in new faith ventures. The ministry of others, both laity and clergy, who are not noted in any such articles is also to be celebrated for they, too, have been faithful in teaching others in a variety of ministries.

The preparation of students for teaching can take on wide implications beyond the topics or themes for any individual teaching session or class. The hope of any teacher, at whatever level of ministry, is that he or she may make a difference in the lives of students who, in turn, will invest their lives in a variety of ways yet to be disclosed. In this respect, teaching embraces a hope yet to be fulfilled in the lives of students. One's teaching is just one small part in the larger ministry of the Holy Spirit in the hearts, souls, minds, and bodies of students, who bless one's teaching with their participation. The mutuality of teaching also suggests that teachers need to be open to what they can learn from their students as well as what they can hope to contribute to their students. Teachers need to be prepared to model a teachable spirit that can influence their students to embrace the same in their learning.

Preparation of Content

In *Principles and Practices of Christian Education,* I explore in some detail aspects of both educational content and methods that are essential in the preparation of teaching content. My effort here is to draw from that previous work key considerations for the process of planning to teach. The content for teaching can take on a vast variety of forms. In 1983, Lee Shulman proposed a model for the reasoning and action of teachers that considers the place of educational content. He identified six areas that serve to connect the preparation for teaching with actual instruction and subsequent evaluation (which will respectively be explored in chapters 2 and 3). The six areas are: the teacher's own comprehension of the subject matter; the transformation of that subject into teaching material; the act of instruction; evaluation of that teaching; reflection of what transpired; and new comprehension of both the subject matter and the pedagogical process.[20] The first two areas relate to the preparation of the content, but they cannot be divorced from the instruction itself, along with the evaluation, reflection, and comprehension of teaching that can follow. What can help a teacher choose from the realm of content possibilities? Several principles can be offered.

First, the teacher needs to gain a sense of ownership of the content itself, whatever it is. It is important that teachers love what they are teaching. Content divorced from the person and work of the teacher cannot be communicated with the passion students need for their own motivation in appropriating or at least wrestling with the content. With content I have taught before on a number of occasions, ownership is only secured when I have intentionally revisited the material and allowed it to connect on various levels with my own life and ministry in new ways. Revisitation calls the teacher to revise or reshape the material, adding and subtracting where necessary and tailoring the material to the

anticipated group of learners. Any content, even in a published curriculum, calls for adaptation in relation to the distinctive context, the teacher who is teaching, and the recip-
ients of the content shared. Revisitation also calls for
rethinking the significance of the content for the journey a
particular group has experienced together up to that point.
This will vary greatly from year to year and in relation to a
variety of contextual factors that will be identified below in
a discussion of the preparation of the context. The ownership and love of the content allow for the expression of enthusiasm in relation to one's teaching and the potential integration of cognitive, affective, and behavioral learning by
students.

Second, the teacher is to consider how the proposed content relates to what the students may already know or need
to know about a particular area. This calls for clarity in
preparing content. The consideration of the goals or objectives of proposed teaching can help clarify direction and the
relationship to other areas of work and life. The work of Elliot Eisner in *The Educational Imagination* is particularly
helpful in understanding how objectives can serve teachers
in their preparation. Eisner makes a distinction among objectives that include behavioral, problem-solving, and expressive objectives. Behavioral objectives specify behaviors
that participants will be expected to demonstrate at the conclusion of a teaching session. Problem-solving objectives
pose a problem or raise a question that participants can solve
in a variety of ways that encourage their exploration and in-
genuity. Expressive objectives foster the imagination of participants through the free expression of their creativity without specifying measurable outcomes or specific problems
to address.[21] The identification of objectives helps provide
clarity for one's teaching in preparation, but the variety of
objectives as Eisner outlines them serves to allow for flexibility and a recognition of the variety of learnings that are
possible. A steady and exclusive diet of behavioral objectives

can squelch the development of the students' critical and creative abilities that problem-solving and expressive objectives nurture.

Third, preparation of the content can include learning experiences that tap into the creativity and critical abilities of both the teacher and the students or participants. The content needs to take on a life of itself. In his ministry of religious education, Abraham Heschel "taught that religion begins with a question and that theology begins with a problem."[22] Wrestling with questions and problems calls for the creative energies of teachers and students along with the inspiration of the creative and life-giving Spirit of God, who hovers over the ebb and flow of teaching and learning. But what holds true for religious and theological education also applies to the whole spectrum of learning that characterizes education in its various contemporary expressions. The content of teaching is to both inform and form students in key areas of study that serve to increase their knowledge, skills, and sensitivities. But the content also can foster the process of transformation in their lives in relation to values, attitudes, and aspects of character that impact all of life. These transformative dimensions of learning often are initiated with the posing of a question or a problem from either the teacher or the students. Abraham Heschel's most common response in class was, "Is that the real question?"[23] The additional questions I might pose for students are: How so? Tell me more. What more might be considered? Why or why not is that the case? Such inquiry can foster the creative and critical energies of students in dealing with teaching content.

Preparation of the Context

The contours of the context for teaching provide a vast array of factors that can impinge on the plans formulated for instruction. How can teachers make some choices from this array for any particular session or event? The teacher can consider the wider context of the world that students confront and global realities. The immediate context is the actual setting in which teaching occurs, the where and when of the teaching along with all the environmental particulars of that setting. Teachers provide both human and material resources with which the students will interact during instruction. A plan serves to orchestrate all of these in ways that contribute to learning. Choices must be made that make sense for what students will encounter in the time they spend with the teacher. With the transformation of the subject into teachable material, as Shulman notes, the teacher needs to consider the context in which the teaching will actually occur. The preparation of the context can serve to demonstrate care for those who will participate and care for the reception of the content.

One key dimension of the context is the welcoming atmosphere or ambiance of the setting. Teachers can plan for how students will be welcomed and initiated into the learning. The use of participants' names and a setting that provides for as much comfort as feasible can facilitate the forming of a personal relationship with participants so that they can settle into the experience and be open to new possibilities. Some educators refer to this preparation as the formation of a learning community that responds to different stimuli in the setting. The lighting, temperature, and sitting arrangements can communicate what is valued to the participants. Materials used for presentation need to be seen and heard if participants are to perceive and respond. Equipment should be tested, and any audiovisual or media presentations should be previewed. In planning I also recommend that teachers consider options that allow for contingencies such as the failure of any technologies used. I ask for the feedback of participants as a necessary check on any well-devised plans that for a variety of reasons may not be functional in a particular setting. For example, I have on occasion resorted to writing on a chalkboard when my carefully outlined overhead transparencies could not be projected because both bulbs in an overhead projector were blown. My usual practice is to arrange a room at least half an hour prior to a class if it is available. This allows time for planning alternative components if some problem should be evident.

A key teaching ability is flexibility when conditions are less than ideal. Remember, the Holy Spirit may have plans other than those in a teacher's lesson plan. While teaching in an inner-city neighborhood, our class break was interrupted when a local merchant who had been shot in a robbery attempt at the corner store entered the building. Thank God two nurses were in attendance to provide emergency first aid while we waited for arrival of an ambulance. The merchant's life was saved. A number of students visited the merchant and his family while he was hospitalized. He came to a vital faith in Jesus Christ as a result of their witnessing and the ministry of care he received. The second half of the class understandably departed from my lesson plan to include prayer for the merchant and discussion of how Christians responded to the realities of violence in an urban setting.

When several years later I was recounting this incident in another class, a student collapsed in what appeared to be a stroke. By God's providence, two different nurses again were present in the class and medical emergency care was administered. The lesson plan was again changed to allow for prayer and debriefing of the whole experience as students shared their feelings and vulnerabilities. I am cautious regarding when and where I share these two accounts of a change in lesson plans, but recommend that teachers be aware that, in God's plan, curriculum may shift as a result of contextual factors beyond our human control. In this, we recognize our partnership with God. An example of that partnership is the opportunity to work with teaching assistants in some of my teaching work. The reflections of one of those assistants, Mark Fountain, is helpful in recalling this second incident of a crisis in the classroom:

> A memorable event transpired in the class that I will always remember. Although far from the curriculum, this incident became an extraordinary example of interpretive education within the context of a formal community of learning. During one class session, a middle-aged student began to lose consciousness and collapsed on her desk. The response of the class was immediate, as we attempted to respond to one of the more existential extreme moments of our shared time together.
>
> We had all grown fond of this student, so her distress created an especially quick set of responses. Two class members, who were nurses, helped to care for the student. In the meantime, an emergency medical unit was called, and the family was contacted. Several of us went to the hospital to meet the student's husband and offer any additional help. Others stayed in class and prayed for the unfolding situation. As it turned out the student recovered and returned to class, and to good health.
>
> Reviewing this event as a class became an extraordinary exercise in interpretive Christian education, and the practice of reflecting. The professor made time in the class to reflect on all that had happened. For me it served as a living metaphor of how existential issues such as life, death, illness and fear can suddenly intrude upon our faith and, by extension, the more controlled setting of formal Christian education.
>
> In addition, this experience also revealed to me the value of cultivating an atmosphere of educational community. Because the class had been designed as a relational environment, the incident, although alarming, did not seem foreign or out of character. Cooperation rather than competition characterized the class. Consequently, when a crisis visited our group, certain values were used by God's grace to address the situation. Some students prayed, others exercised specialized skills, everyone responded according to their faith

45

perspective and "interpreted" the event according to different shades of meaning. During our final evaluation, many students considered this event to be one, among several, key moments of learning during the fall semester of 1994. It was, in the most direct way, an interpretive educational experience.[24]

Conclusion

In *Principles and Practices of Christian Education,* I outline eight teaching skills that are associated with effective learning from the work of Joel Davitz that are also helpful in considering the preparation for teaching explored in this chapter.[25] Those eight skills are clarity of communication, use of a variety of methods, enthusiasm, a task orientation, student involvement, a varied level of discourse, use of appropriate praise and criticism, and the capacity for self-analysis. All of these skills enhance the preparation of the teacher, students, content, and context for teaching. A teacher cannot precisely plan to use enthusiasm or praise and criticism without a potential loss of integrity and spontaneity in actual instruction. An exception is providing feedback on the students' previous efforts or reflecting on previous sessions or questions posed. These eight skills can be developed with practice and serve to incarnate care in the preparation for teaching that can potentially transform students, communities, and the wider society. An in-depth discussion of these skills for the evaluation of teaching is explored in chapter 3. But the fruit of preparation comes in the actual instruction, which is the topic of chapter 2. As with the Brussels sprouts, what we serve on the metaphorical table of our teaching can be greatly enhanced by our devotion to the preparation considered in this first chapter. Such devotion supports teaching as a gift of love we offer to God and others.

2

Instruction

After the careful preparation suggested in chapter 1, the teacher is confronted with the moment of truth, when the actual teaching begins. All that was planned and anticipated is now brought into reality as the teacher encounters the students or participants who have gathered for the event. I propose a metaphor for understanding this second phase of teaching from the musical arts. Though the culinary arts emphasize the place of actual presentation, as my son a culinary artist in his own right occasionally reminds me, the musical arts allow for more play. They pose the challenge of orchestration directly in relation to the activities of teachers throughout the time they spend with students.

In the introduction, I proposed the three elements of *prelude, lude,* and *postlude* for consideration in understanding teaching. The *prelude* comprises those initial movements that engage students and introduce the teaching content on a particular occasion. The prelude sets the stage for what will follow. The *lude* designates the major teaching movements that are presented or played by the teacher. These teaching movements can be further divided by interludes. Interludes allow times for silence, reflection, or dialogue in relation to the teaching content. The *postlude* brings the teaching movements to a conclusion or closure and includes elements of student response that encourage the actual transfer of learning to contexts outside the immediate setting. The *postlude* also anticipates what will follow in the sequence of teaching.

Interlude: Why *Lude?*

The choice of the word *lude* is justifiably questionable. Why coin such a term?[1] My choice relates to a common practice in churches that use a printed order of worship. One typically notes a prelude and a postlude at the beginning and end of the printed order, suggesting something before and after a *lude,* but never noting the *lude* itself. When I was a child and youth, I assumed a *lude* must exist if elements both preceded and followed it. This question about the *lude* is one that I had growing up while regularly participating in worship services at a local Baptist church in Brooklyn, New York. This question may also have been piqued by the fact that Saturday nights I often assisted my father, who was a deacon, in printing the worship bulletin at the church office. My task was to place blotter sheets between each mimeographed bulletin that my dad would pass through the machine with every turn of its handle. Therefore, every Sunday morning I had a particular interest in carefully examining every word of the bulletin. I hoped that none of the words had been smudged. This curiosity about words and interest in the *lude* also relates to my childhood interest in wordplay and wondering what may be missing in any situation. If there is a prelude and a postlude, why not a *lude?* Was something, in fact, missing?

Because of my fascination with teaching, which goes back to my first volunteer teaching experience with a kindergarten class at my local church's Sunday school when I was a senior in high school, I wondered what might be missing in the ministry of teaching. After all that I put my Sunday school teachers through during my childhood and adolescent years, I thought I owed others something in return by teaching a children's class. I can still remember that when asked by my sixth-grade Sunday school teacher to recite my favorite Bible verse, I would regularly share John 11:35, "Jesus wept." If really pressed to do more, I would recite 1 Thessalonians 5:16 or 17. I also sang in the church choir during my high school years and therefore was more aware of the prelude and postlude that Louise Ritts, our choir director and church organist, played each week. All of these experiences in my local church influenced my interest in and curiosity about teaching and its vital relationship to the total Christian ministry.

The missing element of the *lude* in relation to teaching did not make sense to me until I began my doctoral studies at Columbia University's Teachers College. In a teaching course I learned that for many years research on teaching had focused on the presage and context variables of teaching, those factors that set the stage for teaching in terms of the characteristics of teachers, learners, the curriculum, and the classroom context. Research had also focused on the product variables of teaching in terms of immediate and long-term effects. But what for many years was missing in this research was any direct interest in and study of the process variables of teaching, often referred to as the "black box," which remained out of the purview of researchers. For me, some of the missing *lude* or link in teaching related to the joy and passion that needed to be recovered in the process of teaching. The experience of joy is what can distinguish the process of teaching for Christians. That joy was related to the personal association I had with music and the connection between worship and education with worship being central to my model of Christian education.[2]

The word *lude* is actually derived from the Latin *ludere*, which means "to play." This is not to suggest that instruction is only amusing or laughable, but that the teacher, like a musician or an artist, plays out different teaching moves in the effort to teach others. The word also suggests that play, or even "Godly play," in a Christian setting is crucial to effective teaching.[3] The *lude* and corresponding interludes in any teaching event provide occasions for a playful dealing with the universal or perennial questions of human life as well as the particular or everyday questions. In relation to the possible confusion of the synonyms, *lude* and *lewd*, I have come to realize that teaching is too often viewed negatively in U.S. society due to the general embrace of a pragmatic educational philosophy. Pragmatism stresses the "how to's" of teaching strictly out of a practical interest. Teaching is often seen in popular culture as lewd in the sense of being laughable, ludicrous, or even absurd. The popular negative perception of teaching is captured in the statement, "If you can't do, you teach, and if you can't teach, you teach about teaching." As one who teaches and teaches about teaching, I refute that statement. But certainly the potential of negative perceptions and outcomes will always remain with teaching. Teaching itself is risky business, as James 3:1 suggests: "Not many of you should become teachers, my brothers and sisters, for you know that we who teach will be judged with greater strictness." But that negative potential and perception should not deter teachers from relying on God's grace and making their best efforts so that teaching can be a source of joy, life, and passion that makes a difference for students, teachers, and the wider community.

Lude certainly is an awkward term to coin. But its meaning comes into focus in relation to the prelude and postlude of a worship experience. Corporate worship can touch the depths of the human heart with wonder and awe. Teaching at its best can foster a sense of wonder and awe about God and the amazing variety of God's creation. As noted in chapter 1, Richard Baxter, a prominent seventeenth-century English Presbyterian minister, observed in his *Autobiography*:

"I afterward perceived that education is God's ordinary way for the conveyance of his grace, and ought no more to be set in opposition to the Spirit than the preaching of the Word."[4] Through the work of the Holy Spirit teaching can become a vehicle of God's grace, restoring a sense of wonder and joy.

My hope for teaching relates to what happens in Christian worship, where the heart, soul, mind, and strength of persons are renewed by the Holy Spirit. Historically, I also perceive that survival and renewal in faith communities have always been dependent on a vital connection between worship and education. This occurred for the Hebrews in the case of the synagogue, which wed together worship and education—a tradition that continues in Jewish communities that honor the role of the rabbi, the worship leader who is essentially a teacher, and in the ministry of the cantor, who leads the congregation in singing God's Word and praises.

During the Reformation Martin Luther emphasized teaching in the congregation. He wrote catechisms for the instruction of children and their parents. He also stressed the key role of music as a means of passing on the faith to the rising generations. Today's increased interest in music and the arts as media for instruction parallels this development during the Middle Ages. Whereas the Middle Ages represented a preliterate society, in some ways we are entering a postliterate society that relies to a greater extent on the media to communicate key teachings and values. All this brings me to propose the awkward term *lude* to encourage others to consider the missing elements of teaching. These missing elements, if recovered, can restore a sense of joy and wonder that Richard Baxter suggested is God's ordinary way of conveying grace to humankind.

The appeal to the musical arts in this chapter considers teaching as a performance, with the human performers themselves as part of the actual musical presentation. In fact, we can identify teachers as the conductors orchestrating their classrooms or other teaching settings. A popular comparison has suggested seeing teachers as frustrated musical performers who find a captive audience in their classrooms. But the limits of a musical performance metaphor become apparent in attempting to equate teaching with merely entertaining. In the media-saturated culture of the United States, which tends toward entertaining "ourselves to death," diligence is necessary to distinguish teaching from entertainment.[5] While various media are an important vehicle for effective teaching in our culture, the content message of teaching too readily gets lost in adapting teaching to the latest technologies or styles of presentation. Current modes of communication certainly provide a means by which to "hook" students, but the sustained impact of teaching should also be considered in any discussion of instruction. With an exclusive emphasis on entertainment, teachers and students may lose sight of the perennial questions that call for serious grappling with life issues. But such serious grappling ought not exclude the place of enthusiasm and joy that all can experience in effective instruction.

Instruction and Its Place

Teachers initially need to consider the nature of instruction itself if they hope to instruct students. They also need to explore where their ministry includes any other dimensions of learning beyond what is commonly understood as instruction. In *Foundational Issues in Christian Education,* I propose a definition of instruction and compare it with both training and nurture. *Instruction* is education that deals with unpredictable situations. It can be a transforming element of education that emphasizes renewal and change in response to changing situations in society and a consideration of any discontinuities with the past. *Training* is education that deals with predictable, replicable situations. Training is a conserving element of education that emphasizes continuities with the past and the passing on of an unchanging heritage. It is conserving in the sense of maintaining traditional patterns and values over time. *Nurture* involves love, nourishment, and spiritual direction or formation. Nurture, by its very nature, requires a vital and intimate relationship and interaction with others.[6]

What, then, is education, and how is it related to teaching? I define *education* as the process of sharing content with persons in the context of their community and society. The process of education can take on various forms that are formal, nonformal, and informal in character. Formal education occurs in a school setting or system. An example of formal education is the teaching that takes place in a church or Sunday school class. Nonformal education occurs in planned and structured settings outside formal schools. An example of nonformal education is the interaction of persons in a Bible study group that meets regularly in a home. Informal education occurs in unplanned and occasional relationships throughout the life experience. An example of informal education is the learning that occurs between children and parents in the everyday course of living together.

These forms vary primarily with the context of interaction between those who teach and those who learn from others. In each of the contexts (formal, nonformal, and informal), instruction, training, and nurture may occur. In addition, all three dimensions of education (training, instruction, and nurture) can be the focus of teaching, but in this work I focus particularly on instruction that holds the possibility of *transforming* persons in a teaching ministry. The ministry of training relates to the process of *informing* students or participants, and supports continuities with the past. The ministry of nurture relates to the process of *forming* persons, and sustains relationships and a sense of community.[7] A holistic vision of education calls for addressing the information, formation, and transformation of persons. Though instruction primarily focuses on transformation, it cannot ignore the complementary processes of information and formation in the lives of persons. The process of defining terms is helpful for the analysis, precision, and form of education, but should not distract one from the synthesis, creativity, and freedom that is also essential for teaching. The elements of synthesis, creativity, and freedom encourage participants to search for and discover truth and wisdom.

Both order and ardor are necessary in the Christian life and in the ministry of teaching. As teachers we have various gifts in the areas of order and ardor that reflect particular aspects of our personality and experience. Cultural factors also affect distinctive perceptions of order and ardor. As in other areas of human service, no easy formulas exist for how best to teach, but basic definitions and guidelines are shared that require application, appropriation, and translation to the various settings in which the gift of teaching is exercised. This variety suggests that teaching combines aspects of both art and science, but the artistic considerations are primary when considering the actual craft of instruction. With training and its observable results, the scientific aspects would be primary, with the concern for predictability and replication of learning. In the case of nurture, both artistic and scientific insights apply because each person is distinctive but shares with other persons commonalties discerned through such scientific study as human psychology.

With instruction, a host of variables can be cited that impact the teaching setting. The playful handling or orchestration of these variables requires a craftsmanship that is closely related to artistic creation. No easy formulas exist for how a particular instructional sequence must unfold because of the amazing diversity of teachers and students and contextual variables. The array of choices easily confounds even the most experienced of teachers. But with such choices before them, teachers are called on to embrace those essentials or anchors that in musical terms sustain the beat, melody, or underlying rhythm of their instruction. A cacophony of sounds will not result in clear communication, nor a response that is owned by participants and repeated in other settings. What are the essential elements of effective instruction that sustain a teaching effort while allowing for artistic expression? A consideration of the *prelude, lude,* and *postlude* will help us explore these elements.

The Prelude

All that was identified in chapter 1 in regard to teaching preparation comes to fruition in the actual practice of teaching. The choice of initial content serves to introduce what will follow and reorients persons from the various activities that occur prior to actual instruction. Students come to a session with various concerns and preoccupations. The challenge for the teacher is to refocus their attention on the matters of the day. For example, I consistently arrive in the classroom at least fifteen minutes prior to the beginning of any session. This early arrival is not only for the purpose of setting up the classroom, but also to touch base with students as they arrive. Often conversations held with participants prior to instruction provide a bridge to the instructional content.

Another practice in the setting of a theological school is to have a devotional opening to each class that centers our attention. The leadership for the devotion is shared with members of the class. Students most often relate their sharing to course content or themes from the Christian calendar. This devotional opening allows persons to center and focus on God and their potential response to God in what may be shared. As a means of transition when other persons open the session with a devotion, I make connections from the devotion to the course content. The conscious attention to the opening also provides clues for the closing of the instructional time because a similar or repeated theme for the session's closure can provide coordinated bookends for the content. In settings other than a theological school, teachers need to gather the group of learners and have them center on the themes of the day.

Beyond these initial actions of the teacher, it is helpful to consider the possibility of providing an outline or description so students know where the session is headed. In educational terms, this has been identified as an "advance organizer," which serves to plot out the journey for students. This method is especially helpful for those who need a structure or framework on which to hang their learnings.[8] The advance organizer assumes that the teaching is conceptually organized or at least that a theme or question for the day can be stated and shared as well as received by the participants. The advance organizer serves to outline the major points or themes that the teacher will explore with the participants.[9] To return to the discussion of objectives from chapter 1 and proposed by Eisner, even in the case of problem-solving and expressive objectives that have been formulated, teachers can share these objectives as organizers with participants to guide the time together. The communication of direction and clarification regarding procedures serves to bring all persons onto the same page of the musical score in instruction. With adult participants, the prelude may also include the teacher's direct sharing of the assumptions she or he brings to a particular area of inquiry. This may be important if the teaching event is a one-time encounter with the assembled group. With children and youth, an advance organizer helps build expectation and heighten motivation for what will follow.

In the context of an ongoing group, the prelude builds bridges with what has gone before and what will be coming after the individual instructional session. So the prelude more than sets the stage for the major movements that will be explored in the *lude* of the instruction. The prelude also establishes the bridges over which the participants are being invited to venture. In musical terms, the prelude functions as an overture, an opening to the students that introduces the unfolding drama of the complete teaching work that is shared through instruction. The prelude excites the imagination, piques the mind, and engages the will of the participants in ways that anticipate the transformative potentials of the instructional content. A carefully composed prelude invites participation on a number of levels.

A teacher hopes that an effective prelude will gain the attention of participants—a growing challenge in a culture so fascinated with entertainment. Media fascination suggests the need to initially hook participants by introducing an instructional element that grabs their attention and draws them actively. The ultimate threat for teachers is boredom. While engaging the attention of students is a legitimate concern, the fear of boredom, like the fear of failure in general, must not be exclusively determinative of what teachers select for the prelude and other instructional movements. In some cases, students need to acquire a taste for certain content that is only possible over time and with adequate exposure. For example, a study of the meanings of biblical words in their original languages provides new insights for current religious issues under discussion. A taste for such study is acquired over time. Enthusiasm is important, but the issue of integrity ought not be forgotten if the primary interest is "to be trendier than thou" in the choice of teaching content and method. Teachers have to consider the total educational diet if the teaching is to extend beyond a single instructional event. Teachers, on occasion, need to be countercultural in the effort to deal with knowledge, values, or skills that have been ignored or forgotten in the regular learning opportunities of a group.

My approach suggests several levels of risk-taking. For example, in a media-saturated setting, the effort to stress logical analysis and a careful description of the wider context beyond a particular media portrayal can be countercultural in necessary ways. But the use of innovative, media-enhanced instructional forms may also run counter to an existing institutional subculture that has traditionally resisted the use of any mass media. The use of media in this case would be a critical stretch for participants in relating teaching content to students' lives outside the educational experience. The process of discerning these various factors and trade-offs in teaching requires the sharpening of skills over time in the same way that artists hone their skills and are open to a variety of feedback that is provided by observers and participants in their creations.

Patience and perseverance are essential characteristics in the development of the art or craft of instructional style. That style may vary over time and across different settings. One characteristic of style relates to one's openness to receive the contributions of others from the initial movements of instruction. Not attending to these distracts certain students from engaging the content throughout the session. In modeling receptivity to participants, teachers foster a relationship of trust with persons that encourages them to be receptive to what the teacher hopes to share. John 7:14–18 suggests the need for receptivity in the depiction of how people in Jerusalem responded to Jesus' teaching, for he was not expected to have authority. The lack of receptivity to Jesus' teaching is signaled by the question, "How does this man have such learning when he has never been taught?" Wisdom is shared by the unschooled, and the teacher must affirm insights and questions that come from unlikely sources right in the classroom itself.

In the opening moves of the prelude, the teacher signals an openness to participants through eye contact. Scanning the group prior to speaking supports the effort to make some personal contact with the persons assembled. The enthusiasm of the teacher is assessed through the initial verbal and nonverbal cues that are communicated in the first few minutes of instruction. But, again, this must be done with integrity and a genuine desire to share some content of significance for the persons who have invested their time and possible interest in the proposed instruction. Teachers can ask themselves whether they can genuinely welcome those who have come to be instructed. In some cases, the challenge to tap into interests and motivations hidden behind a veneer of hostility and resentment is great. What may help teachers at this point is to put themselves in the place of participants. One way I have found to do this is by regularly praying for my students as a means by which to gain perspective on their situation and to connect with their spoken and unspoken concerns. Silent prayer can also be practiced while launching out in instruction, bringing to God concerns that have been revealed in the initial welcome of persons to the setting.

By way of summary, the invitation given in the prelude draws participants into a shared search for and discovery of truth. This assumes that there is, in fact, truth and wisdom to discover in the process of teaching and learning. For Christians, this represents a faith stance that affirms that in Christ are hidden all the treasures of wisdom and knowledge (Col. 2:3), and that teachers who are Christian directly support others in their search for wisdom and knowledge that connects with life. But the prelude just sets the stage for the *lude* that follows.

The *Lude*

The *lude* represents the major movements of the instructional effort. These major movements may have been outlined in the advance organizer shared with the prelude, or they emerge in an unfolding process of joint discovery or disclosure. Various means signal to participants when a new section or shift in the movements occurs. The numeration of points is one obvious way, as is the posing of a question.

In addition, the use of physical transitions in the case of having students move to another part of a room or to a different learning center alert learners to modal shifts. One matter of concern in relation to the *lude* is its organization related to the three elements of the content, the persons, or the context of the instruction. Logical, psychological, and contextual ordering are respectively related to these three elements. These ways of organizing instruction represent ideal types, but a combination of concerns that complement the primary structure for teaching also is considered. This parallels the presence of major and minor chords that are embedded in musical compositions. The key of a musical selection makes a difference in how the piece is played, heard, and received.

Teachers need to realize that the underlying structure of instruction can be organized around a variety of educational concerns. My proposed educational trinity of content, persons, and context is just one possible framework to guide such choices. The emphasis on content that is most often, though not exclusively, dealing with cognitive concepts would suggest the organization of instruction using a logical order. A logical order is primarily concerned with sequence of learnings as perceived and received by persons who may be neophytes in an area of academic work. Such neophytes are provided with the basic language, questions, issues, and perspectives inherent to a field of study or inquiry. In the case of more advanced learners, a logical ordering of instruction requires the development of one's arguments or perspective with adequate evidence or illustration. Various devices such as deductive and inductive reasoning help in presenting the case and striving to convince or excite participants to deeper levels of thought. When students possess more mature reasoning abilities, the teacher poses problems and raises questions that were not previously discerned in the hope of fostering critical inquiry. This structure assumes the importance of pursuing truth from a variety of sources, but extending the wrestling beyond what is true for me, to what is true for us, to what is true for all.[10] The pursuit of truth requires the engagement of reason and the importance of rationality for human life and community. The danger of the exercise of rationality is the embrace of rationalism that relies solely on reason to comprehend our human situation, which also involves feelings, intentions, values, intuition, motivations, spiritual sensitivities, and even the place of mystery beyond the limits of human reason. While recognizing this danger, teachers can use a logical ordering of instruction that appeals to the cognitive domain of learning.

Related to the logical ordering of instruction, the place of transformation needs to be considered. Transformation in general can be defined as the process of going beyond existing or dominant forms to a new or emergent perspective and reality.[11] Transformation in the cognitive domain supports participants in gaining new perspectives on the world, others, and themselves. Persons are open to having their perspectives and thinking transformed as a result of encountering information that does not fit previously held understandings. This new information creates cognitive dissonance or contradiction that is resolved only by embracing a distinct perspective that has various implications for one's life and commitments. James Loder outlines the various steps that are involved in transforming moments facilitated through instruction. The five steps Loder identifies are conflict in context; interlude for scanning; insight felt with intuitive force; release and repatterning; and interpretation and verification.[12]

The first step of transformation suggests that teachers may help persons by actually posing conflicts and problems or by raising questions that were not previously considered. The teacher is also called on to allow for conflicts to be identified and expressed so that points of incoherence or fragmentation with previously held understandings are made apparent to students.

In step 2, the teacher may suggest sources the students can use in their scanning to discover new vistas. In musical terms, this may suggest the place of improvisation, which is a distinctive of jazz music. The teacher can encourage the students to jazz it up in the sense of being playful in their exploration.

In step 3, the teacher encourages the use of intuition and confirms the emerging insights that students are encouraged to explore. In this step the teacher honors the Spirit's surprise and delight as the students take off on a hunch or insight.

The fourth step, release and repatterning, may require the teacher to provide space and freedom for persons to see and explore alternatives and hunches. At the theological school where I teach, fostering release and repatterning involves encouraging students to discover their own voice and to launch into unexplored areas as they appropriate the heritage of a field and propose new possibilities. On occasion, this requires persons to constructively critique their mentors and move beyond them as a means of gaining some independence prior to exploring points of interdependence within a particular tradition, school, or community.

The fifth step, interpretation and verification, would suggest for the teacher a ministry of confirmation that encourages students to share their discoveries verbally and/or in writing as a public disclosure of their new understandings. This public sharing serves to continue a process of transformation because new problems or conflicts may be revealed, but it also confirms the emerging insights and perspectives. This fifth step serves to complete the personal ownership of transformation in the same way as the public testimony of one's newfound faith fosters a sense of Christian identity.

One example of cognitive ordering from my teaching practice is the use of six-minute summary student presentations of papers. These summaries force the students to cull from their research the essential insights. Students provide a one-page written summary of their final paper to all members of the class as well as share a copy of their full-length paper with a peer. The peer who has read the paper provides an oral response, which is similarly limited to a few minutes. Such a presentation calls for the ownership of insights that are shared with peers. Loder's insights establish a connection between transformation in the area of content considerations and the connections related to the place of persons who themselves are transformed in grasping new insights or understandings.

An emphasis on the persons present for instruction, as distinct from a content-centered focus, results in the priority of psychological ordering of instruction. A psychological ordering uses as a reference the experience of participants and strives to motivate participants by naming and engaging reflection on their experiences. The organization of instruction would have a greater appeal to the affective domain. In addition to the exploration of feelings, the participants explore their values, attitudes, sensitivities, and intuitions on both the personal and communal levels. The appeal to experience that is characteristic of a psychological ordering must be balanced in an instructional setting to foster the examination and discernment of the experience. In an age of uninformed and unexamined experience, this poses a particular challenge, but one that must be engaged to avoid the pooling of impressions that provide no lasting insights for life.

Transformation in the affective domain assumes the interface of the human spirit, a source of passion, with the Holy Spirit. The place of aesthetic transformation or conversion is to be noted as a life-giving possibility for instruction that is spiritual in nature. Aesthetic transformation in Christian faith involves an overwhelming sense of the beauty and majesty of God's love and power often experienced through nature, music, or art shared in teaching settings. A heightened sense of God's holiness and beauty is well captured in Jonathan Edwards' description of his conversion, which increased his awareness of the power and beauty of God:

> Not long after I first began to experience these things, I gave an account to my father of some things that had passed in my mind. I was pretty much affected by the discourse we had together; and when the discourse was ended, I walked abroad alone in a solitary place in my father's pasture, for contemplation. And as I was walking there, and looking upon the sky and clouds, there came into my mind so sweet a sense of the glorious *majesty* and *grace* of God, as I know not how to express.—I seemed to see them both in a sweet conjunction; majesty and meekness joined together: it was a sweet, and gentle, and holy majesty; and also a majestic meekness; an awful sweetness; a high, and great, and holy gentleness.
>
> After this sense of divine things gradually increased, and became more and more lively, and had more of that inward sweetness. The appearance of everything was altered; there seemed to be, as it were, a calm, sweet, cast, or appearance of divine glory, in almost every thing. God's excellency, his wisdom, his purity and love, seemed to appear in every thing: in the sun, moon, and stars; in the clouds and blue sky; in the grass, flowers, trees; in the water and all nature; which used greatly to fix my mind. I often used to sit and view the moon for a long time; and in the day, spent much time in viewing the clouds and the sky, to behold the sweet glory of God in these things; in the meantime, singing forth, with a low voice, my contemplations of the Creator and Redeemer. And scarce any thing, among all the works of nature, was so sweet to me as thunder and lightning; formerly nothing had been so terrible to me. Before, I used to be uncommonly terrified with thunder, and to be struck with terror when I saw a thunderstorm rising; but now, on the contrary, it rejoiced me. I felt God, if I may speak, at the first appearance of a thunder

storm; and used to take the opportunity, at such times, to fix
myself in order to view the clouds, and see the lightnings play,
and hear the majestic and awful voice of God's thunder,
which oftentimes was exceedingly entertaining, leading me
to sweet contemplations of my great and glorious God. While
thus engaged, it always seemed natural for me to sing, or
chant forth my meditations; or, to speak my thoughts in so-
liloquies with a singing voice.[13]

Edwards' description of aesthetic transformation that impacts the religious affections of persons has parallels with a
potential for instruction that deals with the affective domain
when teachers focus on the students' experiences. Teachers
can introduce art, music, and nature into the classroom.
They can hold class in an art museum, studio, or natural setting like the outdoors. Art forms can also include the use of
various media that provide a shared or common experience
that often appeals initially to one's emotions. I describe this
as "gut-level" teaching that addresses participants on a distinctive affective level and elicits deep-down responses to
the instructional elements. The instructional dimension of
the experience and response is reflection that encourages
participants to talk about their reactions or to respond
through a variety of modalities that include art and music.
One example of affective ordering from my teaching practice is the use of the ten-minute film *Why Me?* which portrays the various stages of Dr. Elisabeth Kübler-Ross's stages
of dying. The portrayal is in a humorous, animated format.
Students often comment that the film provides insights at
an emotional level that they did not gain from an academic
reading of Kübler-Ross's book.[14]

The third possibility for structuring the *lude* stresses the
contextual ordering of instruction. An emphasis on the communal, cultural, or sociological order of the instructional
material serves to equip participants for their roles as bear-
ers and reformers of a particular culture or representatives

of certain ideals in the larger society. Persons are encouraged to see the connections between the particular learning setting and their life beyond the immediate context. Priority is placed on the transfer of learning so that participants are transformed from neophytes into active and reflective agents in the world. In this effort, the place of will, intent, and action is emphasized. Transformation in the psychomotor domain involves attention to the behavior of persons and the practice of new behaviors that make a difference. One example of instruction in this domain involves the use of case studies that focus on the actual practice of ministry in a variety of settings. Students at a theological school can explore how they would respond to a variety of issues and problems that typically emerge in parish or congregational settings.

One way of summarizing the possible ordering of the *lude* is to refer to the work of M. Douglas Meeks, who outlines four theories of knowing and learning that have parallels with what is discussed above. In the first way of knowing, we know what we *love*. The affections of persons are primary in this way, as suggested by the description of aesthetic transformation. The virtue of love takes center stage. The learner response to be fostered is that we know in faith because we have been loved by God. In the second way of knowing, we know what we *do*. This way is emphasized in the psychomotor domain, which stresses action. The learner response fostered is that we do what we are in Christ as new creatures. This suggests that our actions should reflect the reality of the new creation, which calls for transformation in our behaviors.

In the third way of knowing, we know what we can *think* in clear and distinct forms. This way is emphasized in the cognitive domain, where persons are encouraged to think new thoughts and to gain new understandings not previously considered. The central preoccupation is thought and the learner response encouraged is that we know God only insofar as God lets Godself be known to us. The transformation anticipated in this way of knowing is dependent on God's revelation and the transformation of the human mind. In the fourth way of knowing, we know what we can *control.* This fourth way is related to contextual ordering. In this case, control is associated with responsibility and accountability along with the engagement of the will and intention of persons. The learner response is that we know in faith because God gives us the power to give up control and give ourselves away in service to God and others.[15] All these ways of knowing relate to the two great commandments found in both Testaments: to love God with all of our heart soul, mind, and strength, and to love our neighbors as ourselves. Fulfilling these commandments in all of life, including the instructional agenda, brings a sense of wholeness and holiness that the Scriptures describe as *shalom.* A wholeness of teaching and learning requires giving attention to all the dimensions of human personal and communal life. Such attention holds the potential of bringing transformation to those who actively engage the instructional process as teachers and learners. Transformation through instruction brings into the human sphere the music of the ages with a melody and harmony that fulfill the deepest longings of the human soul.

Beyond all the particulars of the *lude* analyzed above, the teacher is called on to embody certain principles in his or her instruction. One overarching principle that applies to teaching by Christians is to speak the truth in love (Eph. 4:15). The balance of truth and love is a constant challenge in communication that reflects Christian values. The sharing of the truth requires that persons be encouraged to think critically and creatively. Critical thinking does not mean being cynical in an age of cynicism and destructive critique, but encouraging people to think deeply and broadly about the essential issues of life. This is what Jesus did in his teaching ministry with his disciples. His interactions with Peter, Nicodemus, Martha, and the Samaritan woman at the well come to mind. Such interaction is called for in loving God and God's creation with all of our mind. The sharing of truth in love calls for a sensitivity to persons and the relating of instructional content to their lives. The loving of God and others with all of our heart, soul, and strength applies to the ministry of Christian instructors.

Interludes

Assuming that one way or a combination of ways for ordering instruction has been chosen, the teacher needs to allow for times of transition between the major movements of the teaching itself. These transitions comprise an interlude, a break in the flow of the instruction, and may actually include time for response on the part of participants, who can raise questions or gain clarity about the instructional content or its implications. The effective use of pauses and even silence throughout the instructional element of the *lude* also provides for shorter interludes and a sense of pace and space in what is shared. Research indicates that the quality of student responses improves if the wait time after a teacher's question extends beyond the normal one to three seconds to twenty seconds. When participants respond to questions posed by the instructor, greater control of the direction may be assured in what may unfold in an interlude. But if a teacher is open to whatever questions may be posed by participants, a greater vulnerability arises because the teacher cannot anticipate every question. This greater vulnerability should not be avoided because teaching itself is risky business. Teachers need to admit that there are areas where their knowledge is incomplete. This admission actually signals an opportunity for further investigation and learning. On such occasions I have invited students to explore areas beyond my knowledge or competency in a conjoint effort. This requires that I do my homework and share the results of my study with participants in future contacts either in or out of the instructional setting. If the follow-up occurs in subsequent instructional sessions, another occasion for an interlude is actually provided. The need for interludes in teaching today may reflect the increased role of the media in contemporary life. Today students need breaks, visuals, participation, movement if possible, and the active engagement of the imagination that support the place of interludes in instruction. Recognizing this need, I make extensive use of questions in my teaching practice.

I have often used questions to provide an interlude that fosters integration of material or considers the application of learnings to diverse external situations. The pattern of questions can also serve to unfold different levels of response. For example, in the use of videos, an order of questioning can be used that enhances higher levels of learning. Richard Peace, a specialist in media education, suggests the use of observation questions, feeling questions, reaction questions, and interpretive questions in using a film or video. Samples of these questions from Peace's suggestions are the following:

1. *Observation Questions:* What did you see or hear? What did you notice about the persons, places, or actions?
2. *Feeling Questions:* How did all this make you feel?
3. *Reaction Questions:* Line up the characters—what would you say to them? Enter a scene—what would you do or say? Write a note to one of the characters. If you were to show this film to anyone, who would it be and why? What would you want to say to them?
4. *Interpretive Questions:* What is the vision of life presented in the film? What is the vision of a particular character? What is the vision of the filmmaker? What does the gospel say about this? (Bravo? Boo? Nothing?) Where do we see Christ in this film? Where do we see redemption, salvation, life and its celebration, faith, hope, love, and truth?

In addition to this outline of questions for use with a video or film, it is helpful to think in terms of the various categories of questions that Donald L. Griggs identifies: personal, analytical, and informational. Personal questions are related to a person's own life experience with the intent of guiding students to form values and make decisions. Such questions seek to engage students in the "process of thinking, expressing, and acting on concerns that relate to them personally."[16] Analytical questions involve students in open-ended possibilities that rely on creativity and critical thought. Such questions require students to explore their own thoughts and to express them in dialogue with others. Information questions call for the exercise of the students' memories about specific data or facts. They tend to be more close-ended as compared with the open-ended, analytical questions.[17] The use of all three types of questions serves to enhance the interaction of instruction and to encourage the appropriation and retention of instructional content.

Besides questions posed by the teacher, other instructional elements serve as an interlude in the *lude*. They include questions posed by participants; mini case studies that relate the content to current events; a time period in which students can discuss briefly their thoughts or feelings with others; the use of a story, object, illustration, or example; the application of a concept to a particular setting; the creative use of an excursus or diversion that provides some variety. These examples do not exhaust the possibilities that teachers can use to offer a break in the instruction, much like a commercial break during a television program that in some cases provides a necessary pause before a shift in the action.

Postlude

As noted in the introduction to this chapter, the postlude provides for the conclusion or closure of the instruction and includes elements of student response that encourage the actual transfer of learning to contexts outside the immediate setting. The postlude anticipates what will follow in the sequence of teaching. What I have just done in this text is to repeat an instructional element that was present in the prelude to this chapter, the definition of the postlude. This communication technique applies to teaching as well as writing. I occasionally return to elements I have used to open a class in the conclusion as a way to provide the bookends on the instructional shelf I have constructed. But some shelves are open-ended, and the place of closure may require additional work to which the participants are provocatively invited. In some cases this calls for an assignment that brings home the learning in a variety of ways. The intent is to engage persons intellectually and psychologically so that they will integrate their learning with life outside the instructional setting. The hope is that students will think about and even discuss what was explored in the teaching session with others who were both present and absent from the instruction. In this postlude of thought and discussion, the teacher is available to respond to inquiries and encourage further study and exploration. In fact, the stage is set for a follow-up of learning through the elements emphasized in the postlude. The emotional and intentional crescendo of the postlude can have participants humming or whistling those repeated musical measures long after the original performance. The staying power of the instructional content is enhanced through the postlude.

Several themes relate to the matter of the postlude. They include the review, retention, transfer, and closure of learning, with their corresponding implications for instruction. In relation to review, the teacher presents in the postlude the key concepts, insights, values, attitudes, or skills she or he shared in the particular session. This presentation of key elements assumes the teacher is active and directive in the postlude. But it is also possible for the teacher to be receptive in the postlude by posing questions for participants. One receptive technique I have used with persons is to ask them to write down the one idea or insight they had gained from the particular instruction as they review their notes or engage their short-term memory. Writing down their thoughts in a minute or two allows the more reflective learners to engage the question and to slow down the more verbal learners from immediately responding, thus cutting off the active learning of others. On occasion, I have also asked why persons have written that particular insight and to share with a neighbor. With children and youth this inquiry can explore what they liked best from the session with the hope that they will name something and not respond "nothing" or "I was bored." This inquiry, like with all teaching, is risky. But it does enable instructors to gain some feedback for reviewing what was explored during the actual instructional time.

The retention of learning in the postlude is addressed through the active or receptive mode of teaching. In an active mode the teacher signals what she or he expects the students will retain from the instruction. For example, I might say, "Here is something I want you to remember from all that we have considered today!" or "If there is one thing I hope you will share with others from what we have talked about today it is that. . . ." The enthusiasm the instructor demonstrates for certain content is also likely to make an impression on participants and will more likely be retained. The postlude is an opportunity to provide additional emphasis in order that the students might retain the essentials. Participants are encouraged to consider the implications of the instructional material for themselves and their situations.

The issue of the transfer of learning is explored in the postlude by the application of insights to other settings, persons, or previous understandings. Applications vary, but the effort is made to foster the ownership of learning. Students are encouraged to take what is learned and apply it to both commonplace and novel situations with the clear expectation that such a transfer is possible and appropriate as a response to instruction. Creativity is engaged at this point to imagine what difference, if any, the learning will make. Persons are asked to consider the question of "So what?" Instructors propose a problem, issue, or dilemma that encourages the active transfer of learning.[18] In relation to the transfer of learning, Don Hamacheck suggests that teachers "keep the following guidelines in mind to help such transfer to life experience: (a) connect in-school learning to out-of-school experiences; (b) teach for greater understanding of the 'whys'; and (c) stress underlying principles, generalizations, and applications."[19] The postlude provides the occasion to do this in a direct way that reinforces what persons have learned.

The closure made possible in the postlude provides the opportunity for some culmination of the learning that is intended through instruction. The mention of "some" denotes the open-ended quality of instruction that cannot guarantee the products or results. The intention is that learning will have occurred, but that learning is dependent on the active participation of persons and their ownership of the instructional content. This is the risk of instruction where the teacher offers the instruction, but is never assured of its reception. This recognizes the autonomy of persons and the significant measure of freedom in instruction that is dependent on the choice of persons. The possibility of closure is occasioned by a variety of instructional exercises, such as an exam, paper, or final project in a formal educational setting or a final evaluation, celebration, or time for sharing in more nonformal instruction.

The closure of instruction does suggest an ending, but it also marks a new beginning where persons assume responsibility for what they have learned and a commitment to live in ways consistent with new insights. The Book of James identifies this challenge: "But be doers of the word, and not merely hearers who deceive themselves. For if any are hearers of the word and not doers, they are like those who look

73

at themselves in a mirror; for they look at themselves and, on going away, immediately forget what they were like. But those who look into the perfect law, the law of liberty, and persevere, being not hearers who forget but doers who act—they will be blessed in their doing" (1:22–25). This encouragement to students assumes that Christian teachers have shared the word and the perfect law in a way that students are able to see themselves reflected in the perfect mirror of Jesus Christ. The apostle Paul proposes this standard in 1 Corinthians 11:1: "Be imitators of me, as I am of Christ." The "as" represents a challenge for teachers in their ministries of instruction.

Conclusion

This chapter has explored the second phase of teaching, the phase of instruction, by drawing on a musical metaphor of the prelude, the *lude,* and the postlude. In their instruction teachers are called on to exercise the instruments of their lives in sharing the content of their subjects. This exercise engages the heart, soul, mind, and strength of the teacher. The teacher's sharing of instructional content calls for the best efforts of one called to this ministry while recognizing the gracious working of God's Spirit in the lives of those persons being instructed. A partnership of divine and human instructors is required to avoid a cacophony in a time when discordant sounds are heard from various segments of society. Christian distinctives can make a difference as teachers strive to be in harmony with the music of the spheres begun at creation with the lyrics of God the Father, made most manifest in the melody sounded in the person and work of Jesus the Christ, and graciously orchestrated today in the ministry of the Holy Spirit.

3

Evaluation

The ministry of teaching is incomplete without the third phase, evaluation. Though it is often avoided in the fast-paced world of sound bites and computer networks, evaluation is essential to Christian stewardship of the teaching gifts.[1] The passage from James quoted near the conclusion of chapter 2 mentions the image of a mirror. The mirror is God's Word that is held up to us. By looking in the mirror, we are called to be doers of the Word and not just hearers. Evaluation, like a mirror, helps us discern the nature of our lives, commitments, and values. "Mirrors" of evaluation reflect points of beauty and ugliness in what we are and what we do. The visual arts provide mirrors for viewing our lives. This viewing of ourselves in the mirror can serve as a reality check, with opportunities for affirmation and critique, and is essential for the evaluation of teaching as well as for all of life.

In *Principles and Practices of Christian Education,* I explored the subject of educational evaluation in some detail, but the focus here is on the evaluation of teaching itself and the intended learning that can result from effective teaching.[2] The underlying Christian principle I see operating in teaching is "speaking the truth in love" (Eph. 4:15). Teaching by Christians is best done when the truth in various areas of study and work is shared and when the persons engaged experience: the love of God, others, and themselves. This love involves a love of what one is teaching and learning. This is the case because the love of God includes a love for the world God created. In Philippians 4:8–9, the apostle Paul commands the Christians, those beloved by God, to think and act in certain ways. Their thinking broadly and acting on their thinking is worth noting in relation to teaching: "Finally, beloved, whatever is true, whatever is honorable, whatever is just, whatever is pure, whatever is pleasing, whatever is commendable, if there is any excellence and if there is anything worthy of praise, think about these things. Keep on doing the things that you have learned and received and heard and seen in me, and the God of peace will be with you." All of the values identified in this passage are worthy of careful thought and implementation in action. They also become a basis for evaluation in life and in teaching that seeks to be Christian in character. Naming Christian values that become the basis for evaluation is an important first step in the ongoing process of evaluation in teaching.

Christian Values

What Christian values can be related to the ministry of teaching? Two values that I identify as essential to the underlying Christian principle for teaching are truth and love. The additional values identified in Philippians are honor, justice, purity, pleasantness (related to beauty), commendability, excellence, praise, and peace. A case could be made for each of the values identified by Paul in relation to both teaching and learning that are Christian.

Other perspectives on values for teaching are noteworthy. The consideration of various perspectives helps teachers in the choices they must make. In *Teaching for Christian*

Hearts, Souls and Minds, Locke E. Bowman identifies four "magni-concepts" of the Christian faith that are central for teaching. They include God's love, God's justice, the gospel of Christ (which is God's grace incarnated), and the church as the people of God formed into a faith community. He also names a host of other value concepts that Christians have historically embraced, including truth, faith, joy, hope, righteousness, and peace. In recent curricular materials, he finds covenant, action, life, living, growth, discipleship, and joy to be significant values in the teaching/learning process.[3] In *Vision and Character,* Craig Dykstra cites the work of Plato, who named the virtues of wisdom, temperance, courage, justice, and piety in contrast to Lawrence Kohlberg, who focuses only on justice in fostering moral teaching.[4] Yet another perspective is proposed by Doug Sholl, who identifies a sevenfold pattern of Christian relational content that serves as values for consideration in teaching. Sholl suggests the following pattern: love and justice, truth and faithfulness, forbearance and patience, forgiveness and repentance, edification and encouragement, humility and submission, and prayer and praise.[5] Additional suggestions could be proposed, but each teacher has particular values that either implicitly or explicitly serve to guide his or her thought and practice of teaching. It is important that each Christian teacher consider her or his core values that serve as foundation stones for the practice of teaching and its subsequent evaluation.

My choice is to focus on five values, each of which relate to one of the five tasks of the church I name in my model for Christian education. The five tasks of the church are proclamation, community, service, advocacy, and worship.[6] The corresponding five values for teaching are truth, love, faith, hope, and joy. Related respectively to each of these values is a call to teachers for their consideration in the evaluation of their teaching. I propose the following pairings of Christian values that provide a basis for evaluation of teaching: truth—a call for integrity; love—a call for care; faith—a call for action; hope—a call for courage; and joy—a call for celebration. Each of these values have been identified by others, but they guide me in evaluating my own teaching and that of others. What follows is a consideration of each of these Christian values with their corresponding call in relation to a teaching ministry.

The review of these five values reminds me of an art exhibit I had an opportunity to visit in 1981 at the Museum of Modern Art in New York City.[7] The occasion was the historic display of many of Pablo Picasso's works. My wife, who loves the arts, convinced me to accompany her and a number of our graduate school friends to this event. I admit that I was tempted to sell my ticket for a profit to those who approached us outside the museum entrance. But after entering and viewing the works gathered for this special event, I was delighted I did not yield to my initial temptation to make a quick dollar. I was amazed at the variety of styles and phases of development in Picasso's craft. Each gallery of the museum encompassed a distinct world and way of seeing through the eyes of this modern master of the visual arts. Each style and period of Picasso's work opened up new insights to the world and its realities.

My hope is that Christians who teach will gain new approaches to evaluation of teaching based on each of the five values of truth, love, faith, hope, and joy. Evaluation provides teachers with new angles on their work and helps teachers explore different models for their efforts, just as each period of Picasso's artwork represents a distinct way of viewing the world. Gabriel Moran maintains that "to teach is to show how to live" which requires wrestling with values for living in the world.[8]

Truth: A Call for Integrity

The pursuit of truth is central to teaching. Parker J. Palmer observes that "to teach is to create a space in which the community of truth is practiced."[9] Teachers need to consider whether their efforts are true to their calling, true to the content, persons, and context of their work. Being true to the content refers to the connection between the actual instruction as explored in chapter 2 and that which was designed in the preparation for teaching as considered in chapter 1. Changes may be inevitable in what is planned in advance of actual instruction, but in evaluation the decisions to revise the plans are revisited and reassessed. A certain degree of flexibility is required in teaching, along with a commitment not to be too readily distracted by the whims of both teachers and students. The decision to stay true to the content outlined in one's plans can also be evaluated in terms of what may have been ignored or overlooked in either the planning for or actual implementation of teaching. Being true to the persons in teaching requires a sensitivity to the actual participants and relating one's teaching to them. To do this teachers must foster the learning of students beyond what they already know, relating new possibilities to their lives outside the instructional setting. Being true to the context refers to the teacher's effort to "contextualize" the instruction by making connections with personal, communal, and societal life beyond the immediate setting. The question of truth is also extended to consideration of the curricular foundations of teaching.

Every teaching session, along with its explicit and implicit curriculum, has a null curriculum.[10] Basically the null curriculum is that which is not taught, with the explicit curriculum referring to what is taught. The implicit curriculum refers to what is more caught by persons than directly taught in the course of instruction. In other words, the explicit curriculum focuses on content—the what and how of teaching; the implicit curriculum addresses the formation of persons—the who and why of teaching in terms of personal agency and purposes; and, the null curriculum is disclosed by considering the wider context—the where and when of teaching. The value of truth in relation to each of these curricula raises the important matter of integrity, where the consistency of messages between the explicit and implicit curricula is evaluated and the justification for the null curriculum is considered.

Integrity generally is defined as wholeness of character. Integrity is derived from the same Latin word from which we get the word *integer.* An integer is a whole number, and for the Christian teacher integrity applies to the wholeness or holiness of one's ministry. This wholeness is best modeled for us as Christians in the teaching ministry of Jesus, who serves as a master teacher. In his teaching Jesus modeled or lived what he taught. He incarnated his message in his life and ministry in all of the settings he encountered.[11] While the role of Jesus as an exemplar for teaching is distinct from our efforts, we as teachers are called on to consider what we are modeling. The apostle Paul captures the sense of this challenge in his words as recorded in 1 Corinthians 11:1: "Be imitators of me, as I am of Christ." This text assumes that teachers serve as models for others to imitate. But there are definite limits to the imitation, which is also dependent on the discernment of students. Imitation is only true in the sense of its worth for others to the extent that the teacher imitates Christ in some way. This places an obligation on Christian teachers to model something of Christ in their ministry. Transformative modeling is only possible to the extent that we abide in Christ and rely on the Holy Spirit to work through and sometimes despite us in our teaching. The potential for transformation encourages us to rely on prayer and spiritual discernment in our teaching. But additional helps are provided for us by exploring in greater depth the question of integrity.

The work of Stephen L. Carter is particularly helpful in exploring the question of integrity. In 1996, Carter wrote a book entitled *(Integrity).*[12] He proposes that integrity requires three steps: "(1) *discerning* what is right and what is wrong; (2) *acting* on what you have discerned, even at personal cost; and (3) *saying openly* that you are acting on your understanding of right and wrong." In other words, integrity involves "the courage of our convictions, the willingness to act and speak in behalf of what we know to be right." For Carter, "The first criterion captures the idea of integrity as requiring a degree of moral reflectiveness. The second criterion brings in the ideal of an integral person as steadfast, which includes the sense of keeping commitments. The third reminds us that a person of integrity is unashamed of doing the right." For Carter, a person of integrity is one "we feel we can trust to do right, to play by the rules, to keep commitments."[13] All that Carter describes relates to teachers in their diverse ministries.

Teachers are called on not only to *discern* what is right and wrong, but to be willing to share the fruits of their moral reflections with others through their teaching. Carter's first criterion for integrity has application to all three phases of teaching: preparation, instruction, and evaluation. The matter of right and wrong relates to the truth and the struggle to discern the truth in a wide variety of areas for human inquiry that is at the heart of teaching. This does not assume that the teacher has a corner on the market of truth or that there may be only one perspective on a particular question under consideration. But it does assume that teachers are responsible to spend time and effort in discerning various problems and issues that confront humanity and the wider creation. For younger students those issues include the matters of sharing or being kind to others. Those are also issues for youth and adults, but on a broader and more comprehensive scale they include ethical convictions, care for the environment, and passing on the continuing heritage of humanity across the generations.

Teachers are called on to *act* in teaching settings in ways that are consistent with what they discern to be right and true. In *Principles and Practices of Christian Education*, I explore the teaching example of Jesus, who lived what he taught.[14] For Christian teachers, the call is to seek to be and become all that they affirm in their teaching, thereby modeling a wholeness and integrity. This also requires of teachers the willingness to admit when their actions are not consistent with their stated or implied values. Teachers can ask to be forgiven when their modeling falls short, which is a reality of the human condition with its sin and contradictions. The recognition of shortcomings can indicate an attempt to consider the matter of integrity on a realistic basis. Carter's second criterion of action relates most directly to the phase of instruction in teaching, but both preparation and evaluation include actions of teachers in relation to their values. The choices a teacher makes in preparing to teach involve an inevitable selection of truths. Not all that is true can be shared in any one teaching session. The implicit risk is that the teacher's selection may unintentionally distort all the truth on a particular subject. The instruction for which a teacher plans and actually implements has limitations. Therefore, it is wise for teachers to clearly indicate the real limits, assumptions, and presumptions they bring for themselves and, if feasible, for their students. Teachers also share in their instruction the necessity for continued inquiry along with possible resources for such further study. In evaluation, teachers are open to the recognition of what was not accomplished and could be improved as well as what subsequent actions can be taken to improve the teaching over time. The consideration of actions assumes a willingness to be true to one's commitments in teaching.

Carter's third criterion of *open expression* of one's commitments requires of teachers a willingness to share why they are doing what they are doing in their teaching. The public disclosure of one's rationale, approach, or philosophy fosters the evaluation of teaching. Such disclosure provides a standard in making explicit the rules, principles, or guidelines that are operative at least at the level of thought and intention if not fully expressed in practice. Lawrence A. Cremin identified the inevitable gap between stated intentions and revealed preferences in education, between aspiration and achievement, between the ideal and the reality.[15] W. E. B. Du Bois in his classic work *The Souls of Black Folk* described this gap in the following way: education is a "necessary combination of the permanent and the contingent— of the ideal and the practical in workable equilibrium"—this "must be in every age and place, a matter of infinite experiment and frequent mistakes."[16] The statement of one's ideals and the implications of these ideals for matters of truth, goodness, and rightness helps frame the painting or set the landscape for what teachers hope will be observed in their teaching practice. Besides the value of truth and its call for integrity, teachers evaluate their teaching practice in relation to love and a call for care. Carter, in drawing on the work of Margaret Farley, suggests that the obligation to love others is at the heart of integrity.[17]

Love: A Call for Care

Love is central to the human community and its perpetuation across the generations. Teaching is one essential medium for the passing on of values to the current and rising generations. Therefore, teaching fosters the experience of love in the human community and the wider creation. How is this possible? The concept of "care" may help teachers make the connection between their ministries and the value or ideal of love that Christians affirm.

Teachers are called on to care for the content they are teaching, the persons whom they are teaching, and the context in which they are teaching. In evaluation, some assessment is made regarding how that care was communicated to participants and embraced by them in their learning. How can we measure care or love as the ultimate Christian virtue within an educational setting? In chapter 2, I defined instruction in relation to transformation. It must be recognized that the basic transformative agent for Christians in the world is the love of God made manifest through the life and death of Jesus Christ. How is this love, experienced in a relationship with Jesus Christ, communicated to persons in the ministries of teaching? Jesus, in fact, gave Christians a new commandment just prior to his death, that we love one another just as he has loved us (John 13:34–35; 15:12). The work of Nel Noddings helps in making some connections between care and teaching in fulfilling Jesus' commandment to love others that include those persons we teach. Teachers can imagine their students asking them what Jesus himself was asked by his disciples during the storm: "Teacher, do you not care that we are perishing?" (Mark 4:38). The place of care is essential in the response of teachers to human need in the storms of life.

Jonas F. Soltis observes that Nel Noddings "insists that the main aim of education should be a moral one, that of nurturing the growth of competent, caring, loving, and lovable persons. To that end she describes in great detail a curriculum organized around centers of care: care for oneself; for intimate others as well as strangers and distant others; for animals, plants, the earth; and for human instruments and ideas."[18] Caregiving is central to the human calling that begins at birth. But it is present even before birth in the connection between the developing child and her or his mother in the womb. This is reflective of God's creation and its wonder as described in Psalm 139:13–16:

> For it was you who formed my inward parts;
>> you knit me together in my mother's womb.
> I praise you, for I am fearfully and wonderfully made.
>> Wonderful are your works;
> that I know very well.

My frame was not hidden from you,
when I was being made in secret,
   intricately woven in the depths of the earth.
Your eyes beheld my unformed substance.
In your book were written
   all the days that were formed for me,
   when none of them as yet existed.

The psalmist describes God's gracious love and abiding care for persons from the very beginnings of life, which provides the basis for our care for each other in life after we are born. The general care for other persons modeled for us in procreation naturally extends to the ministries of teaching across the life span.

Noddings' work is helpful in further delineating how care is communicated through teaching. She identifies four aspects of care that can be evaluated in relationship to teaching. Persons need to be recognized, received, respected, and understood at every stage of their growth and development.[19]

Noddings' first aspect, the recognition of persons, is basic to any form of communication. Teachers communicate the recognition of persons with something as simple as using their names. In addition, teachers recognize persons by remembering aspects of their lives or situations. This recognition is facilitated by the practice of prayer for persons with whom one has a continuing relationship. But even in a one-time encounter, teachers can ask persons their names and use them in conversation. In evaluating one's teaching, the question is asked if persons were recognized and remembered and even thought about after the conclusion of the teaching session.

The reception of persons in teaching, Noddings' second aspect of care, is signaled through a willingness to listen to people, facilitated through approachability. The reception of questions and responses from those taught indicates to participants that they are capable of making contributions that will be received by the teacher. The evaluation of such contributions is also important, with the need to care enough to confront persons when they are wrong or need more information about a particular point. Teachers also ought to accept persons with whom they disagree. The place for thought and dissent is to be valued, allowing students to be convinced rather than coerced into positions espoused by the teacher. Jesus modeled a nonauthoritarian approach while exercising his authority as a teacher. He encouraged others to think for themselves and to grapple with the implications of his teachings for them. In this, he trusted in the power of truth to convince his hearers. Again, there are inherent risks in this stance, but the need is to receive persons with their full capacities for critical and creative thought that matures through normal development across the life span.

The matter of respect, Noddings' third aspect of care, can first be named in relation to differences. In an increasingly pluralistic setting, particularly in terms of multicultural and religious diversity, this is important and calls for diligence. The challenge with this diversity is to find a common ground for interaction and discussion that preserves the place of dialogue. Care is required in respecting those who do not embrace Christian values. This stance regarding persons follows from the affirmation of the worth and value of each individual person as created by God. Many issues divide persons today, and in the face of conflict the need is for decency and civility that respects the dignity of persons. This is a particular challenge when religious and theological differences arise in teaching, with the long history of intolerance and discrimination among religious communities. For example, Christians in some settings need to confront their long history of anti-Semitism, which is a heresy in the light of the fact that Jesus himself was a Jew.

Noddings' fourth aspect of care is understanding. The evaluation of understanding in teaching is communicated through the responses teachers give to students in various interactions. Noddings elaborates on the nature of these responses that demonstrate understanding by describing moral education. Moral education itself includes yet another four components from Noddings' perspective of an ethic of caring. They are modeling, dialogue, practice, and confirmation. Modeling involves showing others how to care in our relations with them. Dialogue requires open-ended interaction and a common search for understanding, empathy, or appreciation. Practice calls for opportunities for persons to gain skills in caregiving and attitudes of caring that foster cooperative relationships. Confirmation for Noddings engages what Martin Buber defined as "an act of affirming and encouraging the best in others."[20] These components of care foster understanding that extends beyond the interpersonal encounter between the teacher and individual students to include the development of a sense of community among all those within a group assembled for teaching and learning.

Noddings' portrayal may err on the side of affirming the positive aspects of care that can be communicated in teaching without considering the realities of sin that Christians identify in the human situation. But a similar perspective is proposed by Daniel O. Aleshire in his work, *Faithcare*.[21] Aleshire maintains that paying attention to individual persons is an expression of care, love, and nurture in teaching. In order to adequately pay attention to persons, teachers need various lenses to use in viewing people. The lenses draw our attention to what may be important and crucial for certain individuals and not for others. Just as Pablo Picasso used different lenses to represent reality in distinct periods of his art, so the teacher is called on to evaluate or assess students from various perspectives in understanding them. Such an effort is essential to the affirmation of persons.

In addition to the perspectives of Noddings and Aleshire, the challenge teachers face is to evaluate performance and grade students in formal school settings. This evaluative process assumes some standard of evaluation and comparison of persons. This comparison can include competition as well as cooperation. The other factor that impinges on the realities of teaching is the presence of conflict and the expression of thoughts, attitudes, and actions that are false, wrong, or limited from the perspective of the teacher's experience and expertise. In this case, the caring response is to confront the students whose behavior or perspective is in need of correction. It is not a caring response to have students remain in their ignorance or illusion. Honest assessment is important in evaluating students. Constructive criticism is central to the task of teaching. Teachers need to remember that conflicts are not often resolved with a quick fix. Also, teachers must recognize that they might well be mistaken in their assessment. Teachers must be open to reconsider their assessment as well as work with students to improve their learning and gain new insights.

As identified at the beginning of this chapter, the underlying Christian principle for the evaluation of teaching is "speaking the truth in love." What follows from this principle is the emphasis on the two values of truth and love in evaluation and their corresponding calls for integrity and care. This chapter on evaluation has given prominence to the essential place of integrity and care in teaching. The two primary values of truth and love serve as the two central portraits in the gallery of teaching in the museum of Christian ministries. But the additional values of faith, hope, and joy are worth considering. They serve as complements to the two primary paintings teachers consider in evaluation. They are secondary works that provide an expanded perspective for viewing teaching in its variety of expressions.

Faith: A Call for Action

The linking of faith with action may be questioned, unless one takes the perspective espoused by the writer of the New Testament Book of James. In this book, the value of faith is closely linked with one's deeds or actions. This also, of course, characterized the life and teaching ministry of Jesus of Nazareth, who incarnated faithfulness in action. In relation to teaching, the call for diligent action assumes that the activities of teaching are linked in some way with the activities of learning on the part of participants. Whereas teaching requires actions in the process of instruction initiated by a teacher, learning requires the actions of students. But students may or may not actively engage in the learning process. In *Principles and Practices of Christian Education,* I maintain that the evaluation of teaching should primarily focus on its character as a process and a task and only secondarily on the products or achievement of learning by students who may not want to learn.[22] This is the case because teachers cannot guarantee that learning has occurred without the active participation and ownership of the process by students themselves. This means that teaching at its best is always a risky ministry that calls for diligence and commitment along with a flexibility to reach persons who have a variety of learning styles and dispositions. What, then, are teachers to do in evaluating the fruits of their efforts if the products of teaching are so dependent on the active engagement of students? One immediate response is to strive to gain the cooperation of students in a variety of ways so the teaching effort can result in their learning. In this effort, teachers are to recognize that multiple intelligences serve to support a variety of creative responses to their actions to help other persons learn.[23]

In *Principles and Practices of Christian Education,* I described a number of skills in teaching that provide a basis for the evaluation of teaching. These were briefly named in the conclusion of chapter 1 as a way to encourage diligence in the preparation for instruction, but here they will receive further discussion in considering evaluation.[24] The eight skills, as originally identified by Joel R. Davitz, can be observed in teaching and provide a basis for evaluating the actions of teachers. Paying attention to the specific action of teachers is essential because, as Gabriel Moran advocates, the grounding of the meaning of teaching can be found "in ordinary, earthy, bodily action."[25] The action of Jesus as teacher will serve to illustrate each of the eight skills that Davitz identifies.

The first skill of teaching that can be evaluated in terms of the action of teachers is clarity of communication. Clarity is required in relation to both the instructional content that is shared and the procedures to be followed in learning. Instructional content is shared and repeated in a variety of ways so that participants grasp the key concepts or perspectives that the teacher is attempting to communicate. Clarity of communication supports the retention of content if material is presented on the level of comprehension of the persons involved. The repetition of this material, without erring on the side of redundancy, fosters retention of what persons learn. In relation to procedures, teachers share with participants the stated purposes, goals, and objectives of the instruction as a means to encourage ownership. Being explicit about the boundaries of the instruction by clearly naming the limits, assumptions, and presumptions of the material presented gives students a framework for exploring their own perspectives. Jesus demonstrated this skill by making explicit his truth-claims and teaching with authority (Mark 1:21–22).

The second skill is flexibility or the ability to use a variety of teaching methods. With all that a teacher prepares, she or he must recognize that the actual setting for instruction may present factors not anticipated earlier. In light of this reality, an openness is called for that compensates for change without losing sight of the original intentions and purposes of the session. In evaluation, the teacher reviews whether some of the opportunities for changes were taken and were also appropriate. Discernment is necessary to avoid the whims of both students and teachers. Flexibility sometimes signals avoidance of key areas of learning that should not be passed over with the temptation to follow every lead for a shift in the stated agenda. Using a variety of teaching methods increases the possibility that the participants will be able to maintain concentration and avoid the ever present danger of boredom. The use of variety also demonstrates recognition that there are diverse learning styles in any assembled group that provide distinct entry points for the appropriation of the instructional content.[26] Robert Stein points out that Jesus used a variety of methods, including overstatement (Luke 14:26), hyperbole (Mark 10:24–25), pun (Matt. 23:23–24), simile (Matt. 10:16), metaphor (Matt. 5:13–16), proverb (Matt. 6:22), riddle (Mark 14:58), paradox (Luke 14:11), a fortiori statement (Matt. 7:9–11), irony (Luke 12:16–20), questions (Mark 8:27–32), parabolic action (Luke 19:1–6), poetry (Luke 16:10), and numerous parables.[27]

The third skill that can be evaluated and nurtured is enthusiasm. Whereas an enthusiastic teacher elicits learning, evaluation requires an equal concern for integrity. Enthusiasm must focus on the tasks of learning and teaching along with the direct recognition of any noteworthy contributions of the participants that the teacher may not have anticipated. Jesus was enthusiastic in securing the attention of others. He was direct with such persons as Nicodemus and the Samaritan woman at the well as described in John 2 and 3. One technique I use to engender appropriate enthusiasm in preparing to teach is to review material I have previously presented. This review enables me to personally reorganize the content, making additions and deletions and seeking to develop connections with current events in the lives of participants. The enthusiasm of the teacher is contagious if the instructional content is owned by the teacher in new ways. This ownership requires diligence in the preparation for teaching as explored in chapter 1. In a similar way, diligence in the evaluation of teaching provides new possibilities for future presentations.

A fourth skill is the maintenance of a task orientation in teaching. Effective teachers are able to keep students focused on the tasks of learning. For example, Jesus made explicit his charge to his disciples and their tasks (Matt. 10:1–42). With the ever present interest in entertainment today, the danger is to lose sight of the ultimate and sometimes elusive goal of learning. The teacher models this focus on tasks and encourages concentrated efforts on the part of participants. A sensitivity to persons in terms of care is important in the ministry of teaching, but an equal concern for the content and its potential transformative impact is required. The focus on task is the complementary skill to flexibility. In this maintenance of a task orientation, the teacher provides feedback to students regarding their progress in relation to the assigned tasks and reminds them of the ultimate goals of their efforts.

The ability to involve students in the teaching–learning process is the fifth skill. This involvement includes intellectual, psychological, and, when appropriate, physical responses of participants. Jesus encouraged his students to think for themselves and to wrestle with their commitments (John 6:60–69). The action of teachers is to foster the action of participants with the proviso that the action alone is not the sole component of learning. Action must be complemented by reflection that fosters appropriation or ownership of the learning. This total involvement of persons encourages the transfer of learning to other situations beyond the immediate instructional setting. In evaluation, participants reflect on and assess the levels of their involvement and suggest alternatives that may have improved their engagement with the instructional content. This skill and its evaluation foster the formation of persons as self-directed learners who have learned how to learn in other settings.

A sixth skill for teaching and subsequent evaluation is that of varying the level of discourse. This variety is evident in the methods that Jesus used as cited by Stein above. Discourse can be at the level of facts, explanations, evaluative judgments, justifications, critical analyses and syntheses, concrete realities, and abstract conceptualizations. Discernment is required in terms of the developmental level of participants and what combination of discourse elements can be grasped, but variety encourages creative and critical responses on the part of students. Variety also serves to connect the instructional content with realities outside the immediate setting. It fosters appropriation of the content at deeper levels of understanding and application than would otherwise be possible. By varying the level of discourse, teachers avoid evoking a rote response from participants.

Davitz identifies the appropriate use of praise and criticism as a seventh skill contributing to learning and subject to evaluation. In Matthew 16, we find examples of Jesus' responses to Peter. Jesus both praised or blessed Peter (v. 17) and criticized or cursed him (v. 23). As was the case with enthusiasm, this skill must be tempered with the concern for integrity in teaching. The praise shared with participants must be genuine and appropriate to the instruction. This is a real concern in an age of manipulation. The criticism teachers offer to their students must be constructive, particularly in a critical and cynical age that readily dismisses others through negative critique. In my teaching practice I tend to err on the side of affirmation or praise because of the steady stream of destructive criticism that many persons have encountered prior to entering graduate school. This affirmation centers on students as persons, with criticism reserved for their performance or work. With criticism, it is necessary for teachers to suggest alternatives and to provide suggestions and, when feasible, opportunities for improvement in subsequent efforts.

An eighth skill that can be practiced and is therefore subject to evaluation is a "metaskill." A metaskill transcends other categories and is viewed as deserving special emphasis in one's consideration. This metaskill is a capacity for self-analysis and self-evaluation. This skill is evident even at the close of Jesus' earthly ministry and at the time of his greatest trial in the garden of Gethsemane (Matt. 26:39). The effective teacher is capable of pursuing continuous self-study and -analysis so that her or his actions improve over time. This requires an integrity, a modeling of openness to transformation. Teachers hope for transformation in the lives of their students. This hope applies to themselves as well in the process of instruction. This metaskill requires a vulnerability that has its risks. But the risks are worth taking in the effort of fostering the processes of sanctification and mutual edification in teaching that strives to be Christian in character.

The exploration of these eight skills outlines possibilities for the evaluation of the actions of teachers who recognize their continued discipleship in service of the Master Teacher, Jesus the Christ. Stewardship of our gifts of teaching requires a commitment to evaluate our actions. This is required of those who have received a call to teach and who step out in faith.

Hope: A Call for Courage

Hope is essential to the efforts of all teachers. The late Brazilian educator Paulo Freire pointed out the need for education in hope: "One of the tasks of the progressive educator . . . is to unveil opportunities for hope, no matter what the obstacles be. We need critical hope the way a fish needs unpolluted water."[28] The risks of teaching are such that no teacher can guarantee that his or her best efforts will result in the hoped for learning on the part of participants given the freedom granted to them. The careful preparation for instruction and the implementation of those plans provide the opportunity for learning, but no assurance that all the teacher's expectations will be met at the conclusion of the teaching effort. Courage is called for to enter the instructional setting with the variety of factors that impact the actual achievement of learning by participants. The transformation that is anticipated in instruction requires the gracious working of God, for which the Christian teacher hopes and prays will occur. The realization of the objectives identified in the preparation of content awaits the assessment of both teachers and students after the instruction has concluded. A practice I follow in my teaching is to provide an occasion for evaluation in which participants provide feedback regarding the purposes, goals, and objectives that have been identified from the beginning of the effort. The process of evaluation itself calls for vulnerability and openness on the part of teachers to receive constructive criticism in the hope of improving future instruction. Not unlike a painter poised before a blank canvas with a brush filled with pigment, the teacher stands before students with the hope that what will emerge will be recognizable as a creation worthy of the effort of all participants.

One concrete example of this occurred in my local church during a Christian education intergenerational event. A visiting sculptor created a clay portrait of the crucified Christ. While sculpturing, he was accompanied by music that encouraged observation and reflection. It was a moving and transformative event for the various persons who were present. The visiting artist reminded us that he could not predict how this creation would compare with other efforts or how it would impact us as observers. The experience of this educational event moved me to renewed appreciation for the sacrifice that Jesus made for me in his crucifixion and death. The session also reminded me of what my calling was in becoming a disciple of Jesus for life and the life after death.

Maxine Greene in *Teacher as Stranger* provides a number of key insights for understanding the kind of courage required in teaching. Effective teaching calls for a degree of vulnerability some would rather avoid. Greene points out that teachers must choose and act even in the face of uncertainty that calls for their courage. They cannot predict what every person will do during and after the occasion for instruction. This follows from the perspective that teachers recognize the dignity of persons and grant a certain degree of freedom and autonomy to students that varies with their level of maturity. Teachers also recognize that it is in wonder and questioning that learning begins.[29] The encounter in teaching requires the choice of teachers to risk engagement and a vulnerability to invite participants to do the same in the hope of experiencing transformation. The choice of response is extended to participants so that they, too, exercise their God-given freedom and become responsible agents in their world.

Caring enough to confront students calls for courage in teaching. I have regularly recommended David Augsburger's *Caring Enough to Confront* to my educational students who have had to address conflict and various problems in their teaching ministries.[30] The care that love demands in relation to teaching can also find expression in the willingness to confront persons, situations, and institutions when change is required. Confrontation and the change it anticipates calls for courage on the part of teachers, who may prefer not to rock the boat. But the words of one great teacher of the church can help in gaining perspective. Saint Augustine wrote, "Hope has two lovely daughters, anger and courage. Anger at the way things are, and courage to see that they need not remain as they are."[31] Teachers are called to have courage in addressing situations both inside and outside the instructional setting. This is a dimension of their prophetic and priestly ministry to others with their hope that transformation can occur. As Augustine suggests, courage and anger are related. In my discussion I have stressed courage, yet anger is not to be forgotten. Anger is not often associated with teaching, but anger can be expressed in relation to injustice and a host of evils that plague humankind. Teachers express outrage in their ministries through advocacy by denouncing the destroyers of hope. Nevertheless, the Book of James provides helpful advice regarding the expression of outrage and anger that applies to teaching: "Everyone should be quick to listen, slow to speak, and slow to become angry" (James 1:19). Being slow to speak and slow to become angry does require reflection before the appropriate expression of outrage that sustains hope for a better future. That future anticipates the joy experienced in God for all of humanity and the entire creation as it awaits with eager longing for the revealing of the children of God (Rom. 8:19).

Joy: A Call for Celebration

The experience of joy is too often uncommon in the ministry of some teachers. The concept of biblical covenant in Christian faith recognizes the place of both weal and woe, of both joy and despair in human life. Joy or weal in life is the basis for celebration and the expression of creativity that honors the gift of life itself. Despair or woe in life is the basis for lamentation. The place of lamentation is not be forgotten in the ministry of teaching. But joy found in God overcomes the losses, disappointments, and pains of life that are identified in lamentation. This is the message of the Christian gospel and a message that can be sounded and seen in teaching. This was also the message of the prophet Habakkuk: "Though the fig tree does not blossom, and no fruit is on the vines, though the produce of the olive fails and the fields yield no food, though the flock is cut off from the fold and there is no herd in the stalls, yet I will rejoice in the LORD; I will exult in the God of my salvation" (Hab. 3:17–18).

Teachers can update this prophetic insight: "Though the test results are poor and no great papers are written, though the lesson plans fail and the curriculum needs extensive revision, though the students are absent, yet I will rejoice in the Lord, I will be joyful in God my Savior." Despite our best efforts, the anticipated transformation may not be evident in our teaching ministry. But a source of joy transcends the immediate results in terms of God's presence in the work and in the lives of those whom we teach. This is the basis for our celebration.

Celebration in teaching can also encourage us to explore creative options that we as teachers or our students will engage in instruction. Creating space for imaginative expression releases the energies of participants and provides new perspective on problems and issues under consideration. By honoring the place of celebration, teachers foster a sense of wonder and awe in the instructional process. Learning may begin with wonder and joy as well as end with these Christian virtues. Louis Mackey observes that "Thought and action must be held together in existence by passion."[32] For me, the passion closest to the heart of God is the passion of joy that calls for our celebration in teaching and in all of life. Teaching that communicates that joy holds the potential of enabling persons to connect their thoughts and actions, thereby experiencing transformation.

Conclusion

The analysis of various values in this chapter may lead one to think that they can work in isolation from each other. This cannot be the case. Given the underlying principle of "speaking the truth in love," teachers need to consider a holistic vision for their ministry. In teaching one must speak the truth, but if not done in love, truth itself becomes hard and intolerant of others. Likewise, if one is caring for persons in teaching, but neglects to share the truth, love becomes soft and misguided. Both truth and love need to work in partnership. This also holds for the relationship among the other three values of faith, hope, and joy. The call for integrity requires teachers to see the wholeness of their ministries and the relationship among the five Christian values that are basic for evaluation. No easy formulas exist for making this possible in teaching. Therefore, we as teachers are called to rely on the gracious working of the Spirit of Christ and to a diligence in our evaluation as well as in the preparation and instruction we undertake. We are called to work out our salvation with fear and trembling, recognizing that God is at work within us to will and to act according to God's good purpose (Phil. 2:12b–13). Abraham Heschel reminds us that wisdom and art will not save us, but we are accountable to God for the best possible effort in our thinking and creativity as they relate to teaching.[33] This is what I hope is encouraged through attention to the evaluation of teaching explored in this chapter.

Conclusion

Why write a book for Christians about the basics of teaching? I trust the answer to that question is now clear to my readers. But it is worth repeating in this conclusion. Christians are called to effective stewardship of their spiritual gifts, including gifts for teaching. By attending with diligence and grace to the Preparation, Instruction, and Evaluation of their work (the themes of chapters 1, 2, and 3, respectively), teachers can think about and practice teaching in effective ways. They can put the PIE on the metaphorical table of their ministry as they invite others to sit and feast together.

Teachers who are Christian are called to recognize their partnership with the Triune God. They have the resources of God the Educator, the example of Jesus the Exemplar, and the power of the Spirit the Tutor to instruct in transformative ways beyond the limits of human effectiveness.[1]

A partnership with God encourages teachers to have a stance of humility as well as expectancy. Humility is called for in recognizing the responsibilities, costs, and potential agony of teaching if learning does not occur. Expectancy is called for in recognizing the privileges, rewards, and potential ecstasy of teaching when learning tutored by the Holy Spirit transforms the lives of others. This stance places us as Christian teachers between a rock and a hard place. The rock is portrayed for us by the faith in Jesus Christ of disciples like Peter, who boldly taught in Jerusalem after the coming of the Spirit at Pentecost. The hard place is portrayed for us in the real costs of discipleship that Peter and the other followers of Jesus suffered under persecution. Yet there is no better place to be in responding to the call to teach and fulfilling that call with joy.

Notes

Introduction

1. Robert W. Pazmiño, *Principles and Practices of Christian Education: An Evangelical Perspective* (Grand Rapids: Baker, 1992), 118, 168. These three elements were also named in my work, *Foundational Issues in Christian Education: An Introduction in Evangelical Perspective* (Grand Rapids: Baker, 1988), 205, 206, in discussing curricular foundations.

2. A *lude* is a term referring to the major teaching elements or movements that are presented or played by the teacher. These elements can also include interludes that are times for reflection or even silence. These are explored in chapter 2.

3. Iris V. Cully, *The Bible in Christian Education* (Minneapolis: Fortress, 1995), 91.

4. Ibid., 91–92.

5. Maxine Greene, *Teacher as Stranger: Educational Philosophy for the Modern Age* (Belmont, Calif.: Wadsworth, 1973).

Chapter 1

1. For a discussion of aspects of transformative Christian education, see Robert W. Pazmiño, *Latin American Journey: Insights for Christian Education in North America* (Cleveland: United Church Press, 1994), 55–75.

2. The Puritan doctrine of preparation is discussed below in relation to the preparation of the heart for teaching and how that might be accomplished.

3. Those interested in the recipe for these Brussels sprouts will have to wait for the publication of one of my son's cookbooks in the years ahead.

4. The use of the terms *First* and *Second Testaments* is to suggest a renaming

of traditional categories in referring to the Scriptures as a means of facilitating Jewish-Christian dialogue and recognizing Judaism as a living and vital faith expression today. The use of the term *Old* in referring to the Scriptures honored and embraced by Jews has a negative connotation for some that Christians need to consider.

5. See Mary Elizabeth Mullino Moore, *Teaching from the Heart: Theology and Educational Method* (Minneapolis: Fortress, 1991).

6. See Norman Pettit, *The Heart Prepared: Grace and Conversion in Puritan Spiritual Life*, 2nd ed. with a new introduction by David D. Hall (Middletown, Conn.: Wesleyan University Press, 1989).

7. For a discussion of Ezra and Nehemiah, see Pazmiño, *Latin American Journey*, 123–46.

8. This preparation includes the commitment to study foundational issues. In this area, see Robert W. Pazmiño, *Foundational Issues in Christian Education: An Introduction in Evangelical Perspective*, 2nd ed. (Grand Rapids: Baker, 1997).

9. Samuel H. Dresner, ed., *I Asked for Wonder: A Spiritual Anthology*, Abraham Joshua Heschel (New York: Crossroad, 1995), 63.

10. *Spiritual Formation in Theological Education: An Invitation to Participate* (Geneva: Programme on Theological Education, World Council of Churches, 1987), 8.

11. James E. Loder and W. Jim Neihardt, *The Knight's Move: The Relational Logic of the Spirit in Theology and Science* (Colorado Springs: Helmers & Howard, 1992), 2, 21–33.

12. Richard R. Osmer, *A Teachable Spirit: Recovering the Teaching Office in the Church* (Louisville: Westminster/John Knox, 1990), 52.

13. Moore, *Teaching from the Heart*, 212–20.

14. Robin Smith, "Teaching Reverence: A Theological and Educational Necessity," *Christian Education Journal* 15 (Spring 1995): 64–70.

15. Abraham J. Heschel, "The Values of Jewish Education," in *Proceedings of the Rabbinical Assembly of America* 26:29, as cited in Shulamith Reich Elster, "Learning with 'The Other': New Perspectives on Distinctiveness," *Religious Education* 91 (Fall 1996): 571.

16. The organizing principle of connection is discussed in detail in Robert W. Pazmiño, *Principles and Practices of Christian Education: An Evangelical Perspective* (Grand Rapids: Baker, 1992).

17. The place of study and reflection in teaching is discussed in Robert W. Pazmiño, *By What Authority Do We Teach? Sources for Empowering Christian Educators* (Grand Rapids: Baker, 1994), 97–118.

18. As cited by John M. Mulder, "Conversion," in *Harper's Encyclopedia of Religious Education*, ed. Iris V. Cully and Kendig B. Cully (San Francisco: Harper & Row, 1990), 163.

19. "Up and Comers: Fifty Evangelical Leaders 40 and Under," *Christianity Today* 30 (November 11, 1996): 20 recounts the ministries of Danny and Luis Cortes, who were youth active in the Second Spanish Baptist Church of East Harlem, New York.

20. Lee S. Shulman, "Knowledge and Teaching: Foundations of the New

Reform," *Harvard Educational Review* 57 (February 1987): 1–22.

21. Elliot Eisner, *The Educational Imagination: On the Design and Evaluation of School Programs*, 2nd ed. (New York: Macmillan, 1985), 109–25.

22. Reuven Kimelman, "Abraham Joshua Heschel: Our Generation's Teacher in Honor of the Tenth Yahrzeit," *Religion and Intellectual Life* 2 (Winter 1985): 17.

23. Ibid.

24. Mark S. Fountain, "Integrative Paper" (D.Min. project, Andover Newton Theological School, 1997), 21–22.

25. Pazmiño, *Principles and Practices*, 154–57.

Chapter 2

1. I thank a teaching assistant, Lesley Woo, who raised this question for me.

2. See Robert W. Pazmiño, *Principles and Practices of Christian Education* (Grand Rapids: Baker, 1992), 37–57.

3. See Jerome W. Berryman, *Godly Play: An Imaginative Approach to Religious Education* (Minneapolis: Augsburg, 1991).

4. As cited by John H. Mulder, "Conversion," in *Harper's Encyclopedia of Religious Education*, ed. Iris V. Cully and Kendig B. Cully (San Francisco: Harper & Row, 1990), 163. See page 28 of chapter 1.

5. See Neil Postman, *Amusing Ourselves to Death* (New York: Viking, 1985).

6. Robert Pazmiño, *Foundational Issues in Christian Education: An Introduction in Evangelical Perspective*, 2nd ed. (Grand Rapids: Baker, 1997), 46 n. 32.

7. Thomas Groome refers to education that informs, forms, and transforms persons in "Catechesis and Religious Education: Let's Stay Together," *The Living Light* (Fall 1992): 45, but with reference to the minds, values, and lives of persons, respectively.

8. For a discussion of advance organizers, see Bruce Joyce and Marsha Weil with Beverly Showers, *Models of Teaching*, 4th ed. (Boston: Allyn & Bacon, 1992), 181–95.

9. In more open-ended teaching events, this may be problematic, especially if the teaching emerges from the joint exploration and discovery taking place between the teacher and the students.

10. Gabriel Fackre, *The Christian Story: A Pastoral Systematics*, vol. 2, *Authority: Scripture in the Church for the World* (Grand Rapids: Eerdmans, 1987), 212.

11. See my discussion of transformation and transformative Christian education in *Latin American Journey: Insights for Christian Education in North America* (Cleveland: United Church Press, 1994), 55–75.

12. James E. Loder, *The Transforming Moment: Understanding Convictional Experiences*, 2nd ed. (Colorado Springs: Helmers & Howard, 1989), 3–4.

13. Ola Elizabeth Winslow, *Jonathan Edwards: Basic Writings* (New York: New American Library, 1966), 84–85.

14. Elisabeth Kübler-Ross, *On Death and Dying* (New York: Macmillan,

1969).

15. M. Douglas Meeks, "Christian Education and Conversion," in *On The Way: Occasional Papers of the Wisconsin Conference of the United Church of Christ* 4 (Winter 1986–87): 10–17.

16. Donald L. Griggs, *Teaching Teachers to Teach: A Basic Manual for Church Teachers* (Nashville: Abingdon, 1974), 49.

17. Ibid.

18. For a basic discussion of the transfer of learning, see J. Charles Jones, *Learning* (New York: Harcourt, Brace & World, 1967), 126–46.

19. Don Hamacheck, *Psychology in Teaching, Learning, and Growth*, 4th ed. (Boston: Allyn & Bacon, 1990), 473–75, as cited in Klaus Issler and Ronald Habermas, *How We Learn: A Christian Teacher's Guide to Educational Psychology* (Grand Rapids: Baker, 1994), 207 n. 8.

Chapter 3

1. For a discussion of the gift of teaching, see Robert W. Pazmiño, *By What Authority Do We Teach? Sources for Empowering Christian Educators* (Grand Rapids: Baker, 1994), 59–76.

2. Robert W. Pazmiño, *Principles and Practices of Christian Education* (Grand Rapids: Baker, 1992), 145–68.

3. Locke E. Bowman Jr., *Teaching for Christian Hearts, Souls, and Minds: A Constructive, Holistic Approach to Christian Education* (San Francisco: Harper & Row, 1990), 38–43.

4. Craig Dykstra, *Vision and Character: A Christian Educator's Alternative to Kohlberg* (New York: Paulist, 1981), 10.

5. Doug Sholl, "Unity and Uniqueness: A Theology of Christian Relationships," in *Moral Development Foundations: Judeo-Christian Alternatives to Piaget/ Kohlberg*, ed. Donald Joy (Nashville: Abingdon, 1983), 188.

6. For a discussion of these, see Robert W. Pazmiño, *Latin American Journey: Insights for Christian Education in North America* (Cleveland: United Church Press, 1994), 55–75.

7. In chapter 1, I used an example from the culinary arts, in chapter 2 an example from the musical arts, and now in chapter 3, an example from the visual arts, thus supporting the view of teaching as an art.

8. Gabriel Moran, *Showing How: The Act of Teaching* (Valley Forge, Pa.: Trinity Press International, 1997), 219.

9. Parker J. Palmer, *To Know as We Are Known: Education as a Spiritual Journey* (San Francisco: HarperCollins, 1993), xii.

10. These different curricula as proposed by Elliot Eisner in *The Educational Imagination: On the Design and Evaluation of School Programs*, 2nd ed. (New York: Macmillan, 1985), 87–107, are defined and discussed in Pazmiño, *Principles and Practices of Christian Education*, 91–115.

11. See *Principles and Practices of Christian Education*, 128, where I discuss the general principles of Jesus' teaching with implications for practice. The

principle related to integrity is identified as "Jesus lived what he taught."

12. Stephen L. Carter, *(Integrity)* (New York: Basic Books, 1996).

13. Ibid., 7.

14. *Principles and Practices of Christian Education,* 128

15. Lawrence A. Cremin, *Public Education* (New York: Basic Books, 1976), 50.

16. W. E. B. Du Bois, *The Souls of Black Folk* (New York: Bantam Books, 1989), 65. Chapter 6 of this work, entitled "Of the Training of Black Men," is a statement of Du Bois' educational philosophy.

17. Carter, *(Integrity),* 141.

18. Jonas F. Soltis, "Foreword," to *The Challenge to Care in Schools: An Alternative Approach to Education,* by Nel Noddings (New York: Teachers College Press, 1992), vii.

19. Nel Noddings, *The Challenge to Care in Schools: An Alternative Approach to Education* (New York: Teachers College Press, 1992), xi.

20. Ibid., 22–25.

21. Daniel O. Aleshire, *Faithcare: Ministering to All God's People through the Ages of Life* (Philadelphia: Westminster, 1988).

22. See *Principles and Practices of Christian Education,* 154.

23. See the work of Howard Gardner, *Multiple Intelligences: The Theory in Practice* (New York: Basic Books, 1993).

24. Pazmiño, *Principles and Practices of Christian Education,* 154–57. In that work I draw upon the work of Joel R. Davitz (lecture presented at Teachers College, Columbia University, New York, New York, April 25, 1979). Davitz summarized insights gained from research on teaching. I draw and elaborate upon his work in what follows.

25. Moran, *Showing How,* 220.

26. See Marlene D. LeFever, *Learning Styles: Reaching Everyone God Gave You to Teach* (Colorado Springs: David C. Cook, 1995).

27. Robert Stein recounts this variety of Jesus' methods with a host of examples in *The Method and Message of Jesus' Teaching* (Philadelphia: Westminster, 1978).

28. Paulo Freire, *Pedagogy of Hope: Reliving Pedagogy of the Oppressed,* trans. Robert R. Barr (New York: Continuum, 1994), 9.

29. Maxine Greene, *Teacher as Stranger: Educational Philosophy for the Modern Age* (Belmont, Calif.: Wadsworth, 1973), 86, 92, 286, 268. Also see bell hooks, *Teaching to Transgress: Education as the Practice of Freedom* (New York: Routledge, 1994).

30. David Augsburger, *Caring Enough to Confront: How to Understand and Express Your Deepest Feelings toward Others* (Ventura, Calif.: Regal, 1981).

31. As cited in Wilbert J. McKeachie, *Teaching Tips: Strategies, Research, and Theory for College and University Teachers,* 9th ed. (Lexington, Mass.: Heath, 1994), 384. This is the one work I wish I had read before beginning a teaching career.

32. Louis Mackey, "Kierkegaard and the Problem of Existential Philosophy," in *Essays on Kierkegaard,* ed. Jerry H. Gill (Minneapolis: Burgess, 1969), 46.

33. Samuel H. Dresner, *I Asked for Wonder: A Spiritual Anthology: Abraham Joshua Heschel* (New York: Crossroad, 1995), 80.

Conclusion

1. These categories are proposed by Nels F. S. Ferre, *A Theology for Christian Education* (Philadelphia: Westminster, 1967) and discussed in my work *By What Authority Do We Teach?*, 20–29.

Select Bibliography

Bowman, Locke E., Jr. *Teaching for Christian Hearts, Souls and Minds: A Constructive Holistic Approach to Christian Education.* San Francisco: Harper & Row, 1990.

Dresner, Samuel H., ed. *I Asked for Wonder: A Spiritual Anthology, Abraham Joshua Heschel.* New York: Crossroad, 1995.

Foster, Charles R. *The Ministry of the Volunteer Teacher.* Nashville: Abingdon, 1986.

Freire, Paulo. *Pedagogy of Hope: Reliving Pedagogy of the Oppressed.* Translated by Robert R. Barr. New York: Continuum, 1994.

Gangel, Kenneth O., and Howard G. Hendricks, eds. *The Christian Educator's Handbook on Teaching.* Grand Rapids: Baker, 1996.

Greene, Maxine. *Teacher as Stranger: Educational Philosophy for the Modern Age.* Belmont, Calif.: Wadsworth, 1973.

Greenleaf, Robert K. *Teacher as Servant: A Parable.* Newton Centre, Mass.: Robert K. Greenleaf Center and AT&T, 1979.

Griggs, Donald L. *Basic Skills for Church Teachers.* Nashville: Abingdon, 1985.

_____. *Teaching Teachers to Teach: A Basic Manual for Church Teachers.* Nashville: Abingdon, 1974.

Harris, Maria. *Teaching and Religious Imagination: An Essay in the Theology of Teaching.* San Francisco: Harper & Row, 1987.

——. *Women and Teaching: Themes for a Spirituality of Pedagogy.* New York: Paulist Press, 1988.

Hendricks, Howard G. *Teaching to Change Lives.* Portland: Multnomah and Walk Through the Bible Ministries, 1987.

hooks, bell. *Teaching to Transgress: Education as the Practice of Freedom.* New York: Routledge, 1994.

Horne, Herman H. *Teaching Techniques of Jesus: How Jesus Taught.* Grand Rapids: Kregel, 1971.

Joyce, Bruce, Marsha Weil with Beverly Showers. *Models of Teaching.* 4th ed. Boston: Allyn & Bacon, 1992.

LeFever, Marlene D. *Creative Teaching Methods: Be an Effective Christian Teacher.* 2nd ed. Colorado Springs: Cook Ministry Resources, 1996.

——. *Learning Styles: Reaching Everyone God Gave You to Teach.* Colorado Springs: David C. Cook, 1995.

Leypoldt, Martha. *40 Ways to Teach in Groups.* Valley Forge, Pa.: Judson, 1967.

McKeachie, Wilbert J. *Teaching Tips: Strategies, Research, and Theory for College and University Teachers.* 9th ed. Lexington, Mass.: Heath, 1994.

Moore, Mary Elizabeth Mullino. *Teaching from the Heart: Theology and Educational Method.* Minneapolis: Fortress, 1991.

Moran, Gabriel. *Showing How: The Act of Teaching.* Valley Forge, Pa.: Trinity Press International, 1997.

Noddings, Nel. *The Challenge to Care in Schools: An Alternative Approach to Education.* New York: Teachers College Press, 1992.

Osmer, Richard R. *A Teachable Spirit: Recovering the Teaching Office in the Church.* Louisville: Westminster/John Knox, 1990.

Pazmiño, Robert W. *By What Authority Do We Teach? Sources for Empowering Christian Educators.* Grand Rapids: Baker, 1994.

_____. *Principles and Practices of Christian Education: An Evangelical Perspective.* Grand Rapids: Baker, 1992.

Thiessen, Elmer J. *Teaching for Commitment: Liberal Education, Indoctrination and Christian Nurture.* Montreal, Canada: McGill-Queen's University Press, 1993.

Index

of teacher's heart, 22–25
of teacher's mind, 31–33
of teacher's spirit, 25–31
Principles and Practices of Christian Education (Pazmiño),
   9, 40, 46, 75, 82, 89, 103 n. 1, 104 n.16, 105 n.25, n.2, 106
   n.2, n.10, n.11, 107 n.14, n.22, n.24
Problems, 42, 61, 62, 81, 96
Problem-solving objectives, 41
Process, 10, 42, 89
Proclamation, 77
Products, 10, 49
Prophetic tradition, 96
Psychological ordering, 60, 63–65
Psychomotor domain, 66
Postlude, 10, 47–48, 70–74
Products, 10, 49
Puritans, 18, 23, 103 n.2

Questions, 42, 68, 69, 70, 71
   for media discussion, 69

Rationalism, 61
Rationality, 61
Reality, 47, 61
Reason (ing), 40, 60
Reception, 20, 43, 85
Receptivity, 17, 34, 58
Recognition, 85
Redundancy, 90
Reflection, 10, 17, 40, 92
Release, 61, 62
Repatterning, 61, 62
Repetition, 90
Responsibility, 23
Retention, of learning, 71, 90

Robert W. Pazmiño (Ed.D., Columbia University) is Valeria Stone Professor of Christian Education at Andover Newton Theological School. He is the author of a trilogy of books on Christian education: *Foundational Issues in Christian Education, Principles and Practices of Christian Education,* and *By What Authority Do We Teach?*